PATRICIA PAPPS

ANGELS
of the
ZODIAC

Divine Guidance Through
Your Sun Sign

D1563402

Llewellyn Worldwide
Woodbury, Minnesota

About the Author

Patricia Papps (Dorset, UK) has studied angels and practiced meditation and spiritual healing for more than twenty-five years. She is also an illustrator and has produced children's books, magazine illustrations, greetings cards, and stationery.

To Write to the Author

If you wish to contact the author or would like more information about this book, please write to the author in care of Llewellyn Worldwide, and we will forward your request. Both the author and publisher appreciate hearing from you and learning of your enjoyment of this book and how it has helped you. Llewellyn Worldwide cannot guarantee that every letter written to the author can be answered, but all will be forwarded. Please write to:

Patricia Papps
⁄ Llewellyn Worldwide
2143 Wooddale Drive
Woodbury, MN 55125-2989

Please enclose a self-addressed stamped envelope for reply, or $1.00 to cover costs. If outside the USA, enclose an international postal reply coupon.

CONTENTS

Angels of the Zodiac Reference Guide   *v*

Introduction   1

Chapter 1: Aries   7

Chapter 2: Taurus   29

Chapter 3: Gemini   51

Chapter 4: Cancer   75

Chapter 5: Leo   97

Chapter 6: Virgo   121

Chapter 7: Libra   147

Chapter 8: Scorpio   171

Chapter 9: Sagittarius   191

Chapter 10: Capricorn   211

Chapter 11: Aquarius   233

Chapter 12: Pisces   257

Conclusion   281

Appendix   283

FIRST EDITION
First Printing, 2017

Book design by Bob Gaul
Cover design by Kevin R. Brown
Cover image by SuperStock/The Guardian Angel/Wilhelm Von Kaulbach
Editing by Laura Graves

Llewellyn Publications is a registered trademark of Llewellyn Worldwide Ltd.

Library of Congress Cataloging-in-Publication Data
Names: Papps, Patricia, author.
Title: Angels of the Zodiac: divine guidance through your sun sign /
    Patricia Papps.
Description: Woodbury: Llewellyn Worldwide, Ltd, 2017.
Identifiers: LCCN 2017001205 (print) | LCCN 2017006712 (ebook) | ISBN
    9780738750859 | ISBN 9780738751436 (ebook)
Subjects: LCSH: Zodiac. | Angels. | Astrology.
Classification: LCC BF1726 .P367 2017 (print) | LCC BF1726 (ebook) | DDC
    133.5/2—dc23
LC record available at https://lccn.loc.gov/2017001205

Llewellyn Publications
A Division of Llewellyn Worldwide Ltd.
2143 Wooddale Drive
Woodbury, MN 55125-2989
www.llewellyn.com

Printed in the United States of America

Asmodel, the angel of service, helps embrace and understand service to your fellow man.

Lehatiel, the angel of the violet ray, brings new heights of consciousness and spiritual awareness and helps overcome problems.

Anael, the angel of Venus, provides peace and harmony in difficult situations and brings the ray of divine mother to your soul.

Gemini

Pheniel, the angel of transformation, guides you in finding your true spirit.

Tomimiel, the angel of positive thinking, helps you gain a positive attitude to life.

Ambriel, the angel of the yellow ray, assists in healing depression and brings clarity to the mind.

Raphael, the angel of Mercury, helps attain a state of heaven through realisation of the divine light within.

Cancer

Zorial, the angel of imagination, helps you use your imagination wisely and attain a sense of safety and security.

Muriel, the angel of peace, helps you find the true peace of the spirit.

ANGELS OF THE ZODIAC REFERENCE GUIDE

Aries

Machidiel, the angel of renewal and courage, helps bring courage and refreshes your mind when feeling confused.

Teletiel, the angel of the red ray, brings energy and provides patience in difficult situations.

Rahmiel, the angel of love, brings the power of love to your heart and an understanding of altruistic love.

Samael, the angel of Mars, provides harmony and guidance in daily life.

Taurus

Suriel, the angel of beauty, brings understanding to the true meaning of beauty and helps you see the beauty in all you meet.

Sattamiel, the angel of the silver ray, heals hurts, helps overcome negative aspects in life, develops your healing powers, and provides angelic help when changes in life are inevitable.

Gabriel, the angel of the moon, brings spiritual illumination.

Leo

Haniel, angel of joy, develops your heart centre and brings true joy to your soul.

Verchiel, the angel of faith, develops trust and confidence in divine power.

Ariel, the angel of the orange ray, brings optimism and strength of character and resolves distressing situations that unbalance your state of mind.

Michael, angel of the sun, strengthens your mental power, sends healing into the world where there is conflict and strife, and embraces the light within your heart and strengthens this light.

Virgo

Cheial, angel of serenity, brings deep peace and contentment from which serenity can flow.

Betuliel, angel of commitment, embraces commitment to the spiritual path and in learning who you truly are.

Hamaliel, the angel of the blue ray, helps in communicating your true self, brings a positive outlook to your life, provides energy when feeling low, and relieves stress.

Zadkiel, the angel of Mercury, receives messages from the angels and achieves unity between the lower self and the spiritual self.

Libra

Tzorial, the angel of courage, brings courage to your heart.

Zuriel, the angel of harmony, attains true harmony of the spirit.

Masniel, the angel of the green ray, brings balance between the head and the heart, brings hope and insight to difficult situations, and helps you realize your dreams.

Hasdiel, the angel of Venus, develops your talents and radiates divine love.

Scorpio

Hetiel, the angel of creativity, helps you be creative in all aspects of your life.

Barbiel, the angel of compassion, assists with learning the true meaning of compassion.

Acrabiel, the angel of the indigo ray, develops your intuition, restores enthusiasm for living life to the fullest, and brings tranquility when in a stressful state.

Azrael, the angel of Pluto, teaches you the secrets of your spirit and the reasons for your present incarnation.

Sagittarius

Medonial, the angel of caring, assists in finding the true meaning of caring for others.

Chesetiel, the angel of the gold ray, brings prosperity and riches into your life, brings the warmth and energy of the sun to your mind and body, and understands spiritual laws.

Sachiel, the angel of Jupiter, helps you attain unity with the divine light.

Adnachiel, the angel of sacrifice, helps you with the true nature of sacrifice and obtain union with your higher self.

Capricorn

Shenial, the angel of pleasure, assists in understanding the true meaning of pleasure and to experience more pleasure in your life.

Gediel, the angel of the purple ray, provides unity with the higher consciousness and helps balance energy levels.

Uriel, the angel of wisdom, helps you gain divine wisdom.

Cassiel, the angel of Saturn, helps you achieve the life you want and in understanding the lessons you have incarnated to learn.

Aquarius

Gabriel, the angel of happiness, assists in learning the true meaning of happiness and to achieve such happiness in your life.

Deliel, the angel of the magenta ray, helps attain transformation to a true spiritual being and heal old emotional scars enabling you to move forward in life, to lift dark clouds from your soul and bring a new awareness of joy, restoring harmony when things go wrong in your life.

Cambiel, the angel of brotherhood, helps with understanding the mystery of true brotherhood and sending healing love into the world.

Auriel, the angel of Uranus, receives spiritual revelations that lead you to understand spiritual truths.

Pisces

Romiel, the angel of self-confidence, helps you gain self-confidence and in realizing your own unique talents.

Dagymiel, the angel of the turquoise ray, helps with making the right decisions and finding forgiveness.

Barchiel, the angel of mastery, assists in gaining control over disruptive emotions.

Asariel, the angel of Neptune, expands your consciousness and works from your higher self.

INTRODUCTION

Meditations with angels of the zodiac will bring you to new heights of spiritual awareness and answer the questions you have about the spiritual path. The angels will bring healing to your life and raise your consciousness so that you understand the spiritual side of your nature. Within each of us is the spark of the divine light, and the angels can inspire us to develop and embrace this spark so that it grows and radiates throughout the entire being—mind, body, and soul. Developing the divine spark will eventually bring divine illumination, and the angels will be with you to help you achieve such a state of spiritual knowledge and the positive changes it brings to your life.

Angels bring magic to your life for they are working from the divine will and their only wish is for us to be joyous and to live in harmony in our daily lives. They know the secrets of your life and will impart this knowledge to you through meditation when you open yourself to their love and wisdom.

Angels will bring special care and love to the soul for they are working in harmony with the power of your zodiac sign. They will help you to realise your full potential and make your dearest wish come true. Live your dream with angels by your side, for their love and support will inspire you to make your desires a reality.

You can tune in to any angel of a different zodiac sign throughout the year and take advantage of the different energies at varying times of the year. The companionship of angels in your life will truly make miracles occur and you will find that you are experiencing greater happiness, health and prosperity.

Each angel listed has been carefully researched and considered from various sources and in my own meditations with angels. I have been guided to pair the angels with the various lessons of the soul I have detailed here. Angels bring magic into our lives and take care of us, and these angels in particular can help us live more contentedly and peacefully. They will help you develop your full potential as worthwhile and confident human beings. Angels give us their love, and as we give love in return so our spiritual consciousness expands and we broaden our scope to live fulfilled and happy lives.

How to Meditate

Meditation brings a time of tranquility in your routine of the day and puts you in touch with the still, small voice within you. This small voice can guide you to a better way of living if you are unhappy about your life at the moment. Meditation eases out the tension in your soul and body and brings guidance from the divine that will bring magic and miracles into your life. When you meditate, you are in touch with the highest part of you, that part that is one with the divine life, and as such the guidance you receive can only be for your utmost good. With regular practice you will find that your emotions are under your control and that anger, fear, and anxiety melt away in understanding and discernment.

The practice of meditation not only calms the mind and emotions but brings about an expansion of the spirit within you. Meditation opens you to the possibilities of divine illumination and the wisdom and altruistic love they bring to your soul. Each one of us has a light deep within that is part of the divine, and through meditation and the power of the angels this small light will develop and grow so that it illuminates your whole being. This is divine illumination and the expansion of this light awakens the mind to divine thought.

Meditation brings a deep peace to the soul and calmness to the mind that has very beneficial health benefits. When one is at peace your body is relaxed and well balanced and your mind is free from worries and anxieties. You will find that your mind is more under your control and is positive in thought when one practices meditation on a regular basis. Thoughts become clearer and you have the courage to face difficulties with a newfound resolution.

To start your meditation practice, it is a good idea to perform a few rituals to still the mind and let the frets and thoughts of the everyday float away. First, make sure you will not be disturbed: switch off your phones and let whoever you live with know that you don't wish to be disturbed for a while. It is very beneficial to have some sort of an altar you can meditate in front of, as it will focus the mind. It need not be a permanent altar, although it is a good idea to have a place where you regularly meditate. Try and meditate in the same place as this will bring a sense of security and focus for the mind likes regularity.

Keep various things you find spiritual on your altar such as a crystal you feel attuned to and a vase of flowers. You could also have a picture of something that particularly appeals to you and is spiritual in nature. Always have a candle on your altar, as this is an important part of the ritual of meditation. The little candle flame represents the spark within you that is part of the divine. Concentration on the flame will still the mind and prepare it for meditation.

Begin your meditation by making yourself comfortable. You can sit cross-legged on the floor, ensuring your back is straight and that you are well focused. Rest your hands lightly on your knees. If it is uncomfortable for you to sit cross-legged, extend your legs straight in front of you and lean your back up against a wall or item of furniture. You could also sit comfortably in a chair with both feet on the floor and your hands resting in your lap. Being comfortable is the most important thing, as any discomfort can greatly disrupt your concentration. Make sure also that you are warm and have a shawl or a blanket nearby to keep out the chills. Feeling chilly also greatly disrupts the concentration of meditation. It is also a good idea to have a glass of water handy, especially for after the meditation, for to take a few sips of water can ground yourself after the meditation.

When you are comfortable, focus for a few moments on something spiritual such as a crystal, flower, or a picture if you have one. Then light your candle and concentrate on the little flame for a few moments. This little flame represents the light within and reminds you that you are one with the divine.

When you feel ready, imagine yourself in a beautiful garden full of colourful, fragrant flowers and delicate shrubs and trees. There are pools with water lilies and fountains of sparkling water. The sun is shining in a beautiful blue sky, and the birds are singing in the trees. Butterflies flit from flower to flower, and the scene is one of great beauty and harmony. This is the garden of the angels and it gives you a deep pleasure to walk there. Be aware of this pleasure and feel the joy walking in this garden gives you. You feel very happy and relaxed, whatever the circumstances of your life. You feel your soul expanding and opening to the beauty of the scene.

You come to a garden seat overlooking a rose garden and you sit down and contemplate the beautiful roses in front of you. Really imagine their fragrant perfume and their vibrant colours that range from the most delicate pink through yellow, and deep red. You feel very relaxed and at peace with yourself and your life. You also feel very safe and secure. Your guardian angel stands behind you with his/her hands on your shoulders to help you with your meditation. You are now ready to start your chosen meditation.

When you have finished your meditation, there are some closing down rituals you should follow. Your chakra centres open to allow you to absorb the power of the angels during meditation, and these need to be closed down again. Start with your base chakra, at the base of the spine. Imagine a silver cross encircled with light and hold it over the chakra centre for a few moments to seal the centre. Then repeat the process for your second chakra, in the small of your back. Your solar plexus is next, and then your heart centre in the middle of your chest, not over your heart. Next comes your throat centre, followed by your brow centre between your eyebrows. Finally, close down your crown chakra which is on top of your head. When all your chakra centres have been closed down, it is a good idea to take a few sips of water to further ground yourself.

1
Aries

Machidiel, the Angel of Renewal and Courage

Aries arrives when the earth is renewing itself after the winter, and the angel of renewal, Machidiel, is the special angel of the Arien. This angel is also the angel of courage. He will support you as you rethink where you are going in life and what progress you have made on the spiritual path. Just as nature blossoms into new growth in the springtime, Machidiel will bring to your soul the sense of the renewing power of the divine deep within you and will awaken your spirit to the possibilities that come with renewed growth. Machidiel will come to you to help you renew your determination to awaken your soul to the goodness and love of the divine spirit which dwells within you. Machidiel is a lovely angel full of love and kindness who will awaken the spirit within you to all that is good in life and give you the courage to look at your life and see what needs to be rethought.

Machidiel reminds you of your soul's purpose in this incarnation and will lead you to endeavours anew. Renewal brings that quickening of energies, bringing a renewed belief in the strength of the great spirit. As the angel of renewal, Machidiel will help you reaffirm your determination to let go of all that is negative within your soul and allow the light of the divine to shine forth, not only for yourself but for all creation.

Renewal means focusing on your dreams and all that is good in your life, reaffirming your commitment to look afresh at your life, your work, your relationships, and your spiritual aspirations. Machidiel will help you overcome any negative aspects in these areas and will assist you to bring about healing and inspiration. Just as the energies of the earth are at their most potent in spring, so does Machidiel bring a new potency to the soul of the Arien and will help you reaffirm your intention to live your life with joy and peace and with the wisdom of the divine spirit within to bring about positive change in your life.

Machidiel knows the soul of the Arien and will help you put your unique abilities to the greatest positive use. Courage and determination are needed when seeking to start anew, and with the angel's help you will bring about a blossoming of your spirit that can only mean an equal blossoming in your practical life. As you embark on a new year full of dreams and good intentions, Machidiel will be with you all the way to bring your dreams to reality.

Machidiel brings new energy to your soul to bring about those things you have been dreaming of and will assist you to live life afresh and with new vigour. The meditation with him will help you renew those parts of you that are weak or afraid, or where you are lacking in confidence and bring positivity and courage to your emotions and sense of being.

Renewal means looking at your life and seeing where change needs to take place and Machidiel will be with you to support you as you bring about these changes. Change can sometimes be painful, but Machidiel is right beside you to uplift you and whisper words of encouragement. He will give you the realisation that positive change can only bring renewed hope and pleasure to your life. Renewal goes beyond change, for it is an affirmation to seek the highest goodness within your soul that brings a commitment to act from all that is good in your heart.

Meditation with Machidiel will set the way for the three other angel meditations for Aries, starting you on a pathway that will bring joy to your spirit and a blossoming in your life bringing happiness and fulfilment.

Meditation to Find Courage When Feeling Fearful

Prepare yourself for meditation by following the suggestions in the introduction. See a beautiful angel standing in front of you dressed in spring green, the colour of renewal. Machidiel, the angel of renewal, has come to you and he offers you his hands in a gesture of greeting. Take his hands and feel his energy spreading through you.

The spring green light of the angel permeates your entire being, bringing a renewed affirmation to energise that which is good within you. The light of the angel melts away all that is weak, fearful, and negative and leaves you with new courage and ready to live your life to the full taking on all the challenges life has to offer. The melting away of all that is negative allows all that is good within you to affirm itself. Feel your heart centre expanding in the light of the angel; imagine your heart centre aglow with a soft pearly light. See this light spreading out into the world to bring comfort and healing where there is despair. Feel yourself renewed in body, mind, and spirit and know that all that is positive within you is energised and created anew.

Hold this feeling of being uplifted by the spring green light of Machidiel for as long as you feel comfortable then bring your awareness back to your actual surroundings. Thank the angel for his help. Keep a note of any thoughts that come to you during the next few days regarding any problems that perplex you or any questions you have of the spiritual path, for this may well be Machidiel guiding you.

Teletiel, the Angel of the Red Ray

The colour ray of Aries is red and the angel of the red ray, Teletiel, watches over Aries and comes to you dressed in vibrant red, reflecting the energy and vibrancy of the Arien spirit. Teletiel is a powerful angel who brings harmony to the soul and new insights into the deeper meanings of your spirit. He will also renew your energy when you are feeling depleted and bring clear insight into how to live more harmoniously.

Aries brings dynamic power and a restless spirit that can result in a burned-out feeling. Red, the colour of your angel, will bring a renewed vigour to your physical being as well as a refreshed outlook to your mind. Aries is of the element fire and the colour red signifies this at its most powerful. Fire can be dangerous, and the Aries character acting hastily and with their usual enthusiasm can often get their fingers burnt, but Teletiel is always with you to heal and guide you back to a more harmonious way of living.

Our colour angels are there for us every moment of our lives, and Teletiel knows the weaknesses as well as the strong points of the Arien soul. He will lift you up when things are not going as you would wish. Our colour angels are there for us when times are rough and things are not going as we would wish. When you have problems in your life, Teletiel will be there for you to help and neutralise any negative energy. This may be money problems or relationship problems. Whatever it is that causes you distress, Teletiel will be there to heal and bring about a positive conclusion. In your meditation with your colour angel, imagine a symbol or person representing the difficult situation; healing will come to you and the angel will restore harmony to your life.

The Aries personality likes to be in control and can feel threatened when this is not the case. Teletiel will heal any feelings of threat and bring you to an understanding of the situation and a realisation that sometimes it is all right to let go and trust that all is working out for the best for everyone concerned.

The colour red symbolises the passion and exuberance of the Aries spirit, and Teletiel will help you put this passion into action. Red is about action, and the Aries soul inspires others to live life with the same passion and energy the Aries soul displays. Red is also symbolic of initiation and Teletiel will guide you along a spiritual path that is both fulfilling and enlightening.

Meditate with Teletiel when you need a boost of energy and perseverance, and you will feel a great uplifting of your spirits. When things go wrong in your life, he is always by your side to whisper words of encouragement. If you visualise him dressed in red robes beside you, you will immediately feel regenerated even in the most depressing of circumstances. Teletiel knows only too well that the Aries soul lacks patience when circumstances get out of control and he will bring peace to the soul and a realisation that everything has its time and not everyone can act with the same energy and commitment as the Arien soul. This is something that is often difficult for the passionate Arien heart to understand but Teletiel will bring that understanding and a much more forgiving nature that is aware of other people's weaknesses.

The following meditation with Teletiel will bring about a regeneration of your physical energy when you have been overdoing it, as is often the case with Ariens. When your spirits are low, you need the energising radiance of Teletiel and the colour red to set you back on course to fulfil your dreams and accomplish those tasks which you have set for yourself.

The second meditation with Teletiel will bring harmony and healing to distressing situations that you are experiencing. When on the spiritual path it is difficult to keep a spiritual outlook when things are going wrong and causing you distress. Teletiel will bring his harmony and peace to the situation and leave your mind and heart clear to concentrate on the positive aspects of the spiritual path.

The third mediation with Teletiel will work on your spirit to set you on the path of initiation into the higher mysteries of the spirit. Whatever path you choose, the Arien spirit will devote itself to gaining spiritual knowledge with the same passion and energy as you do for all the challenges in your life. You are a passionate personality and Teletiel will help keep you on the path that is best suited to your fiery nature. Once set on the right path, you will pursue it with a commitment and energy that only the Arien nature can display. Teletiel, your colour angel, will be beside you to encourage and guide you as you follow your chosen path. The spiritual path, like any other pathway in life, has its pitfalls and stumbling blocks but Teletiel will guide you round these and regular meditation with him will bring you a clear insight and understanding about which path to follow. The Arien spirit will embrace the challenges that spiritual growth brings and with the help of your angel you will bring both uplifting and inspiration to fellow travellers on the spiritual path.

Meditation to Bring Energy Back to a Depleted Soul

As Aries is a fire sign, a candle flame is a most suitable aid to concentration and contemplation for stilling the mind but you must use what is most comfortable for you.

Teletiel stands before you dressed in robes of fiery red. There is a red glow around your angel, and he extends his arms in a sign of love and welcome to you.

Concentrate on the glowing red and feel this fiery colour permeating every part of your being, not just physical but your mind and soul bodies. Feel this power surging through you energising your tired limbs and uplifting your tired mind. Your angel enfolds you with his love, and the deep warm red colour he radiates revitalises your body, mind, and soul. You feel ready for anything and welcome the challenges that life brings you. Teletiel brings to you understanding and the knowledge that everything has a purpose in life to teach and your lesson is that not everyone can keep up with the Aries energy. You will find yourself being much more patient with people and considerate of those who do not share your opinions. If you have a real problem that needs sorting, ask the angel for his help by visualising something that is symbolic of the situation or a person you are having difficulties with. The angel will be only too ready to help you and you will be surprised how soon harmony is restored to your life.

Teletiel also rekindles in you the feelings of pleasure that is so much part of the Aries character. Know that your angel is with you every moment of every day to help, restore your energy, inspire, and uplift. He never leaves you. Give him your love and thank him for the never-ending encouragement he brings to your life.

Hold the image of Teletiel and the warm red colour for as long as you feel comfortable. Then gently bring your awareness back to your surroundings. Know that the angel is still with you even though you can no longer see him. With regular practice of the meditations with Teletiel you will become more aware of his actual presence. Some people are actually aware of a figure at the edge of their vision and know that this is their special angel.

Meditation to Resolve Difficult Situations

When things go wrong in our lives and cause us anxiety and distress it is not easy to live harmoniously and we often find it difficult to follow the spiritual path. Money problems can prove very difficult to deal with and can cause great anxiety as can relationship problems when they go wrong. Whatever problem you are facing, whatever disaster has happened in your life, you will find it difficult to find the peace meditation can bring you. However, the meditation with Teletiel, the angel of the red ray, focuses on the problem and will bring a sense of balance back to your life. The angel will bring peace and healing to the situation. It is difficult, but trying your best to practice this meditation will go a long way in healing the situation and bringing you the peace of mind that's been so difficult to find.

Sit comfortably and prepare yourself by following the suggestions in the introduction. Before you stands Teletiel, the angel of the red ray, in a shimmering red robe. Feel the red light of the angel enveloping you and permeating every cell of your being. The red ray dissolves any negative feelings you may have regarding the distressing situation. Bring to your mind's eye a symbol of the situation that is causing you anxiety. If it is a relationship problem imagine the person or persons involved and see them enfolded in the red light of the angel. Know that all will be well and healing will come to the situation.

If it is money problems that are causing you anxiety imagine yourself surrounded by gold coins. Feel the red light of the angel enfolding you. The red light permeates your entire being, body, mind, and soul and leaves you feeling enriched and happy. Pick up a handful of gold coins and let them slide through your fingers. Feel the red light of the angel healing your anxiety and know that all will be well.

If it is some other problem that is causing you distress imagine a symbol that represents the problem. Hold this symbol in the red light of the angel and know that a wonderful healing will take place and all problems will sort themselves out in a most positive way. Hold yourself in the red light of the angel and feel relaxed and happy.

When you feel ready bring your attention back to your actual surroundings and take a few deep breaths. Repeat this meditation every day until you feel the situation has righted itself and give thanks to Teletiel for all his support and help.

Meditation to Bring Initiation on the Spiritual Path

Teletiel will help you on your chosen spiritual path and bring enlightenment and a greater understanding of your true purpose in life.

Begin your meditation as suggested in the introduction. Teletiel, the angel of the red ray, stands before you dressed in beautiful red robes and radiating a brilliant red glow. Feel this red glow permeating your body and mind bringing about a new awareness of your inner spirit. The angel holds out his hands to you and you take them and feel the angel's energy and wisdom radiating throughout your entire body and mind. Know that guidance will come as to the best spiritual path for you to follow, one that suits your enthusiastic nature and boundless energy. Know that enlightenment will follow and you can if you wish ask Teletiel any questions you have about the spiritual path.

Answers will come if not immediately, within a short space of time. Initiation on the spiritual path is a very exciting time and with your special Angel beside you, you know that you will discover spiritual truths that will bring you immeasurable joy. Know that you have stepped onto an exciting path, and with your Aries energy you will see it through to joyful fulfilment. Teletiel will be with you to guide you on this path and give you encouragement when you feel disappointed. Contemplate these thoughts with your angel and feel his love for as long as you feel comfortable. Then bring your attention back to your surroundings and give thanks to your angel for the love and help that comes to you.

Regular practice of this meditation will bring about a wonderful opening up of the spiritual world and bring a pathway that suits the Aries nature. Your special colour angel, Teletiel, is always beside you so do ask questions if things get confusing. To do this, you just have to imagine your angel dressed in red standing beside you. It is as simple as that. An answer will always come, so be patient. This is not easy for the Aries temperament that likes answers right away but patience is one of the things one needs to learn on the spiritual path. Keep an angel notebook and jot down ideas and thoughts that come to you. You will be surprised how quickly answers do come.

You have started a wonderful journey on the spiritual path with Teletiel beside you and your Arien nature will respond with all the enthusiasm and energy that so encapsulates your sign.

Rahmiel, the Angel of Love

Love is the soul lesson for Aries and the angel of love, Rahmiel, watches over the Arien personality from the moment of birth until death. Rahmiel is a beautiful angel who loves you unconditionally. His gentle nature will lead you to unconditional love for yourself and for all creation. Such love is difficult to feel but Rahmiel, the angel of love, will bring about a greater wisdom and understanding that will enable you to expand your heart centre and give your love to all creation thereby bringing great joy to your soul.

Love is an important lesson, for it brings one to the very heart of divinity. Rahmiel brings the realisation that divine love is more than the love of human relationships. It is a much deeper and far-reaching love that takes in the whole of creation. Rahmiel will whisper words of encouragement to the Aries soul who is embarking on the spiritual journey and will reveal to that soul the secret of divine love that is the healing balm for all ills.

Meditation with Rahmiel will develop the heart centre and bring about an understanding of the true nature of the soul. He will demonstrate that pure love for all life is the secret waiting to be discovered by every soul who embarks on incarnation. Once divine love manifests in your heart, you will experience untold joy, for it heals all negative emotions such as depression, fear, anxiety, and all the petty hates and jealousies that can do so much damage to the soul. Rahmiel will always be beside you to encourage the Arien soul to positively use those gifts that are particularly yours. Your infectious enthusiasm will bring direction and joy to those souls who cross your path. Rahmiel will guide you to use your gifts wisely.

Aries personalities are prone to charge ahead with so much enthusiasm they leave little time to think through what they are doing. Meditation with Rahmiel will bring about a realisation that you need to stop sometimes and think through what you are doing. Rahmiel will bring a clarity of mind that helps you look before you leap, a common fault of the Arien character.

The lesson of the love that the Aries personality has incarnated to learn is that of sacrifice and the greatest sacrifice for Aries is that of the self will to that of the divine will. Rahmiel will guide the Arien soul to reach this ideal for it will be the most difficult of the lessons that the Arien soul has to learn. Surrender to the divine will means no longer acting entirely for oneself but judging the situation and acting for the best for all concerned. You will know when you are acting rightly, for you will feel a warm glow at your heart centre and a feeling of elation that only connection to the divine can bring. Regular meditation with Rahmiel will bring a peace to the restless Aries personality and will make sacrifice of the will to the divine a much easier goal to achieve. Rahmiel will always be with you to help you when you fall short of your target and will guide you to self-discipline and dedication to the divine within your heart. Once the Aries soul has achieved this self-discipline and the divine love in the heart rules the mind, a wonderful irradiation of the whole being takes place and the soul can no longer live for itself alone but has a deep feeling of responsibility and love towards all life. Your splendid powers of leadership will be used to inspire and guide others and this will bring a great fulfilment to your soul.

Aries is a cardinal sign, indicating love in action and Rahmiel will guide you as to the best course of action for your soul's qualities. Working for charities or where your physical energies can be put to use are the best routes to take for your enthusiasm and energy will make things happen in a most positive way. Rahmiel will help you decide which route to take and meditation with him will set you on a course for life that will bring you the greatest joy and fulfilment. Rahmiel will awaken in you the flame of divine love and this will irradiate your whole being bringing about the transformation of the earth personality into the gold of the great spirit. You will be able to bring new hope and courage to those who are despairing and you will know your life's mission is to bring the word of divine love to all who will listen.

Once divine love has manifested in your heart, you will understand that such a love is nonjudgmental and Rahmiel will celebrate when you no longer stand in judgement of others but understand their weaknesses and fears. Rahmiel will bring this understanding to the Arien heart and your selfless love for all humanity will bring about a union with the divine and inspiration to all who come in contact with you. Being nonjudgmental also means not judging yourself. Accepting your faults and mistakes and understanding the reasons for them will bring you closer to understanding others. We all make mistakes at some time in our lives and the secret is not to get too upset about it. Mistakes help us grow in understanding and can assist us to move forward. Holding on to guilt is very corroding to the soul and will serve no purpose. Learning to let go of guilt will bring about a love for oneself. This is not a selfish love but an understanding of who you really are—a child of the divine Spirit with all the gifts and talents it entails. Forgiving yourself for errors will make it easier to forgive others and will allow divine love to shine through your heart.

Meditation for Love

Sit comfortably and prepare yourself for meditation by following the suggestions in the introduction. Before you stands a beautiful angel clothed in soft pink robes. This is Rahmiel, the angel of love. Feel his love irradiating every cell of your body, enfolding you and warming you. Give him your love in return. Feel yourself surrounded by a comforting pink light and feel a response in your heart centre.

The angel of love melts away all that is selfish, proud, opinionated, and unworthy in your nature until only the pure love of the divine remains. This will bring forth your positive Arien qualities of courage, enthusiasm, determination, compassion, and consoler and inspirer of others. You feel at one with your angel and with the great Spirit. The light and love of the great Spirit will shine through you to comfort and bring new hope and courage to those who are despairing. Your life's mission is seen clearly in the illuminating light of Rahmiel, the angel of love.

Feel this love filling your body and soul and hold this feeling for as long as you feel able. Then bring your awareness back to your surroundings and take a few deep breaths. This is a very powerful meditation with Rahmiel, and the spirit responds with all the enthusiasm of the Arien nature. Be aware of any thoughts that come to you over the next few days as these may well be from Rahmiel.

With regular practice of this meditation you will feel a glowing sensation at your heart centre begin to grow as your spirit responds to the divine. You will feel more at peace for divine love brings a great peace to the soul for one knows there is nothing to fear when held in the love of the divine.

Samael, the Angel of Mars

Aries is ruled by Mars, the planet of fire. It has always been known as the planet of war and destruction. The Arien nature might often bring about disharmony and destruction of some kind upon itself but it is useful to remember that out of war and destruction often come great advances in knowledge and social progress. Samael, the angel of Mars will be close to you at such times when you have brought havoc to your life and will uplift and inspire you to take positive action. The great Spirit always brings something positive out of all negativity and it is a lesson for the Arien to learn that out of negative happenings, the Arien nature will make progress on the spiritual path and learn great insights not only into himself but also about the divine nature in man.

Mars rules the head and intellect, bringing about clear thinking that will mean right action. Samael, angel of Mars, brings clarity to the confused mind and power to the intellect which needs to be fully developed to experience union with the great spirit. Meditation with Samael will work on the intellect and develop the mind in the heart from which springs true altruistic love.

Our thoughts are powerful and bring about negative or positive conditions in our life. What we dwell on we dwell in, so if our thoughts are predominantly negative, our life will reflect such feelings. However if our thoughts are predominantly positive we will on the whole have a pleasant and enjoyable life. We create our life through our thoughts and everything we do or have started with a thought. The circumstances of our lives will reflect our thoughts and the angels will always be with us to steer us in the right direction and help us live life with a positive outlook. Samael will help lessen negative tendencies and turn around negative thoughts into positive thought patterns. The Arien nature tends to be more on the positive side but outbreaks of impulsive action, foolhardiness, and pride can cause great pain and anguish. Samael will come to you in meditation and heal these negative emotions and bring you to a place where you can calm your mind of rash impulses and pride that produce so much misery. The Arien nature is one of vision and creative power, and Samael will help you use these powers for the greatest good.

The power of Mars is found in people who are outstanding workers for social reform or good causes in general. Samael, the angel of Mars, will help you see where your talents lie and will point you in the best direction to fulfil your Arien nature.

Having developed the heart centre and nurtured the divine love with Rahmiel, the angel of love, Samael will show you just how to go about using this power in your everyday life. He will bring the courage of your convictions and having realised the divine spirit within, you will want to develop your life to manifest the altruistic love at your heart centre. The intellect needs to be fully developed so that you can think clearly and have the knowledge of right action and right speech. Samael will develop the mind to be positive and creative and will also give you the ability to cope when things don't go quite according to plan. At such times you need the wisdom of Samael to help you overcome adverse circumstances and have the power to fight for what is right and good.

When Mars is weak in a horoscope there is a tendency for lack of physical energy and a reluctance to keep going when obstacles arise. The meditation with Teletiel, the angel of the red ray, will greatly help in this situation by bringing energy and determination back to the depleted soul and a determination to achieve despite any adverse conditions. On the other hand those with an overabundance of Martian fire will find themselves in hot water many times but Samael will help achieve a harmonious way of living and bring a cooling energy. It is not surprising that most people who achieve any degree of fame or success will have the Martian ray well developed, and Samael will help bring the Martian fire under control, channelled into positive action. Samael will encourage the skills of the Arien personality and indeed, Aries could be called the sign of skill in action.

The Martian energy brings a thirst for knowledge and awakens a desire for occult knowledge which can lead the soul into light or darkness, depending upon whether the knowledge is used altruistically or selfishly. Samael will lead you along the pathway of light to use its knowledge for the most positive of reasons and will encourage you to develop healing abilities. With Samael, the Arien can find hidden depths of knowledge which can be used for the uplifting and healing of mankind. Good thought leads to good action and Samael will help keep your thoughts positive and creative. This is called "the mind in the heart," for your thoughts will respond to the altruistic love you feel in your heart. This love will give your thoughts power to uplift, heal, and console those who are in despair.

Samael is also the bringer of truth and this is something you pursue with all the vigour and determination of the Arien nature. The search for truth is an age old attempt to find the reasons for our life and the reasons for what happens to us. Samael brings answers and you will realise that the love at your heart centre is the key to all the mysteries of the universe.

Meditation for Harmony and Guidance in Your Daily Life

Make yourself comfortable and follow the suggestions for relaxing yourself as detailed in the introduction. See standing before you Samael, the angel of Mars, dressed in a glowing red gown. Feel his power and strength enfolding you. Feel the power of the angel working on your mind and body, bringing about positive thought to bear on your life. Feel also the harmony that Samael brings to your soul and you feel at great peace. He will show you how to deal with any negative conditions in your life and you know that all will be well. Just feel the power of Samael permeating every cell of your being and know that he will be with you to heal and guide you as you go about your daily life. He will bring you answers over the next few days and will bring harmony to your Arien nature.

Hold the feeling of the power of the angel enfolding you for as long as you feel comfortable, then bring your attention back to your surroundings. The meditation with Samael, the angel of Mars, is powerful and regular practice will bring about positive changes in your life. Keep a notebook handy to jot down ideas that come to you over the next few days as these will be messages from the angel. You will realise truths of the spiritual path that will bring you understanding of yourself and your life and your more positive outlook will mean a more harmonious way of living.

Enjoy your life with these special angels watching over you and you will find untold joy and fulfilment and your dreams will become a reality.

2
Taurus

Suriel, the Angel of Beauty

The angel of beauty, whose name is Suriel, is the special angel of Taurus and draws close to the Taurean soul to whisper a very special message: in reality, you are a very beautiful, shining spirit. This is the truth of your being and Suriel, angel of beauty, will help you shine forth your beauty to the world as an expression of the divine light that is at the core of your being. Beauty is the natural state of your spirit and Suriel will show you how to express this beauty, be it a warm smile, an act of kindness, or caring for animals or other human beings. Once you acknowledge the beauty that is divinely yours you will recognise that beauty in other people.

Suriel will bring you the truth that all are connected by the divine spirit. The beauty of the divine spirit shines in everyone and everything that has been created by the divine will. You will be able to look beyond the outward appearances of people and see what is truly divine and beautiful in them. Outer appearances are deceptive and material considerations, but Suriel will help you see the true beauty that shines in everyone hidden by layers of personality and materialism. The beauty of your spirit is beyond comprehension but to be aware of it is to acknowledge the divine within not only in yourself but of every human being no matter what that person chooses to express.

The Taurean nature is highly attuned to beauty in all its forms in the material world, and Suriel will bring a deep understanding of the true nature of all creation. The Taurean spirit can be uplifted by the beauty of a flower, by music, by art, indeed by all that is beautiful in the world and such appreciation can put the Taurean in touch with his/her spirit and bring about a wonderful joy at the sheer pleasure of just being alive. Once you have made contact with Suriel, you will feel a deep need to remove all that is ugly in your life and negative in your soul. Suriel will bring you a deep appreciation of all that is wonderful and beautiful in your life and you will look on the things that you have, be it a relationship, a pet or your home or nature, with a renewed joyfulness at their innate beauty. You will look at people afresh and recognise in them the true beauty of their spirit which is at one with your own spirit. By recognising this beauty of the divine in all you meet and have dealings with, you will find that your relationships will improve and become more positive. Through meditation with Suriel you will find that your life will become more harmonious and your appreciation of all that is beautiful in life will deepen your awareness of the unity of all creation.

Suriel will support you as you look at that which is not so beautiful in your personality. None of us are perfect but the Taurean nature of calmness, patience, and loyalty and your true appreciation of all that is beautiful will lead you to eliminate all that is negative in your soul. Suriel will awaken your desire to know the truth of your being and will lead you to understand the true nature of your spirit. Beauty is an essence that shines forth from within and is not touched by negative conditions of the world. Suriel will inspire you to reach up to the divine and seek the knowledge that only touching the divine can bring. That knowledge is that every single human being shares the same wondrous beauty of spirit, no matter what they choose to develop and communicate. Realising this shared beauty of spirit will bring healing to negative souls and by affirming the truth of the beauty of unity will help others to realise this beauty and unity for themselves. The shining beauty of the spirit is eternal and can never be harmed by outer conditions. Let your beauty shine forth to uplift and heal all you come in contact with and let this beauty heal your own soul and bring you to the realisation that you are truly a beautiful child of the divine.

Taurus occurs at perhaps the loveliest period of the year, when spring is in full bloom and the trees are heavy with blossom. The countryside and gardens are full of the wonderful colour of spring flowers, all enhanced by the wonderful birdsong at this time of year. This is symbolic of some of the finest qualities of the Taurus soul and Suriel will come to you to help you fulfil your soul's desire to make a real contribution to the harmony and pleasure of life.

Meditation to Understand the True Meaning of Beauty

Make yourself comfortable and follow the suggestions for preparing for meditation as detailed in the introduction. See standing before you an angel dressed in beautiful robes of many colours. These colours are very harmonious and can be shades of pink, purple, blues, and greens or whatever your mind imagines. This is Suriel, the angel of beauty, and he welcomes you with a warm greeting. He lifts his hands and directs at you a beautiful ray of pearly light. This light shines right through you, permeating every cell of your being. You feel uplifted and joyful. You know that you are a truly beautiful being and that beauty can illuminate the lives of all you come into contact with. Suriel brings you the realisation that your beauty is the light of the world and shines in every living soul. You feel a determination to look at all that is negative in your soul, and with the help of Suriel you will turn these negative things into all that is positive. A wonderful peace comes over you for you know that this truth means there is nothing to fear in life: you really are a child of the divine and angels look after you. The beauty of your true being brings hope and peace where there is despair and strife. Contemplate these things for as long as you feel comfortable then bring your awareness back to your present surroundings.

Regular practice of this meditation will bring to the Taurus soul a great joy and happiness and will prepare the soul for the meditation with Asmodel, the angel of service, as this is the special lesson Taurus brings.

Asmodel, the Angel of Service

Service is the soul lesson of Taurus which every Taurean has incarnated to learn. The angel of service, Asmodel, is with you always and will guide you and bring you words of encouragement in your chosen tasks and will bring you the realisation of what true service is. Service is giving of your best, giving your soul light to all you meet and helping where help is needed. Asmodel brings the message that true beauty of the spirit is the pure altruistic love at your heart centre.

The Taurean soul is well prepared for service in some form, for your patient and caring personality is ideal for helping people less fortunate than yourself. Asmodel, angel of service, will bring you ideas as to which particular way of service suites your nature best. Service comes from the heart centre and is a giving of your divine light through action. Service comes direct from the divine within you and gives your soul the greatest joy. Through service you recognise the best in people and feel the unity of the divine Spirit that is in all of us. Service is more than just helping; it is caring and sharing the light of your true nature and recognising that nature in others.

Asmodel will help your divine Spirit to shine through the personality to bring healing and peace wherever there are negative conditions. The Taurean nature enjoys pleasure and the service you choose needs to be something that will give you the greatest joy. Once you have made up your mind what kind of service you are going to give nothing will divert you from that path. Taurus is an earth sign of fixed quality, giving a steadiness and an almost rock-like determination to keep going and achieve what you set out to achieve. Asmodel will be with you to help you in your endeavours and will lift you up and give inspiration if you come across difficulties in your chosen path, although your fierce determination will see you through the most obstinate of problems. Asmodel will give you the strength of character to carry out your path of service to the best of your abilities.

There are many forms of service and many Taureans find nursing or some other caring profession most suitable for their kindly natures. It may be that service to animals or children is preferable for you. Whatever is your chosen pathway Asmodel will be right beside you to inspire and help you bring fulfilment to your soul. Service of some kind is what the Taurean soul yearns for and Asmodel will guide you as to the best pathway to follow.

Meditation with Asmodel will open up your heart centre to the light of the divine and will attune you to the divine love of the universe. Service comes from the love in your heart, and that love will develop as you serve until its all empowering nature will radiate throughout your entire being. This love will heal and inspire where there is despair and bring comfort where there is sadness and loneliness. To serve is one of mankind's greatest callings and the Taurean answers that calling with all the determination and steadfastness of his/her nature.

Meditation to Understand and Embrace Service to Mankind

Sit comfortably and prepare yourself for meditation as suggested in the introduction. Imagine a beautiful angel standing in front of you dressed in golden robes. This is Asmodel, the angel of service, and he radiates you with his golden light. Feel this light permeating every cell of your being, lifting you above the material matters of everyday. This light illuminates your mind and brings inspiration as to your ideal way of service. This light also expands your heart centre and you feel full of love for all creation. The light at your heart centre spreads throughout your entire being and fills your whole body and mind. Contemplate this love and know that it will shine on all you come into contact with, illuminating their lives and bringing hope and joy where there is sorrow. This love will also shine on your own life and bring healing where there is any negative condition. Contemplate these things in the light of the angel and feel his love for you flowing to you and enfolding you. Send him your love in return and when you feel ready bring your consciousness back to your actual surroundings.

Regular practice of this meditation will bring a deep joy to the heart of the Taurean and help you on your road of service. Keep an angel notebook handy to jot down any ideas that come to you for these may be angel guidance.

Lehatiel, Angel of the Violet Ray

The angel of the violet ray is Lehatial, an angel of extreme love and gentleness and also of immense power. He watches over the Taurus soul and will bring you energy when you are feeling depleted, sort out problems that are distressing you and bring you spiritual awareness.

The Taurus personality can be very obstinate and does not give in easily, either to problems that stand in your way or to a depletion in energy from doing too much. Lehatiel, the angel of the violet ray, will bring you a warm energy that will refresh a tired mind and body and will bring you an understanding that sometimes it is all right to let go of things and allow others to do their bit. As a Taurean you will find this very hard to do but Lehatiel will bring a softening of the Taurean will and help you to give opportunities to others. As an earth sign the feelings of Taureans go deep and despite your kindly placid nature you can feel deep hurt at times, but Lehatiel will bring his healing balm to soothe such hurts and bring an understanding of other's points of view.

The violet ray is the ray of beauty and ceremony, both of which are at the heart of every Taurean soul. It is also the ray of power and one of the lessons that Taureans have incarnated to learn is the value of money. Money of course symbolises material power and you may well experience the acquisition or loss of money or property. With the help of Lehatiel you will gradually overcome such problems and will come to understand the responsibility and spiritual significance of money.

As an earth sign Taureans often find it difficult to rise above the earthly level of consciousness, but with the help of Lehatiel your spirit will soar to new heights that will bring you untold understanding and joy.

Taureans appreciate the beauty and creative power of ritual and ceremony and will be drawn to spiritual concepts that incorporate such in their worship. Lehatiel will lead you to your ideal path of spiritual unfoldment where the beauty and power of the ritual involved will have an almost magical effect in awakening your higher consciousness. With your instinct for order and rhythm you will begin to understand spiritual law and Lehatiel will help you put into practice this law in material issues. Whilst remaining your Taurean self of essentially a practical and capable nature, the angel will help you cease to be limited purely by worldly values and will help you to base your dealings with people on true spiritual values. Lehatiel will help your own power to increase to the extent that wherever you go you bring the gift of restoring confidence, comfort, healing, and bringing order out of chaos. This is the true lesson of the earth element and Lehatiel will be beside you all the way to help you learn and lift you up when you feel yourself weakening.

When things are not going right for you or you have problems that seem insurmountable, then Lehatiel will come to you to help you overcome and put things right. Your colour angel is with you all through your life and will be there when you need him, to lift you up above worldly problems and help you see such things from a spiritual viewpoint. All problems can teach us a spiritual lesson, and Lehatiel will help you understand when things go wrong in your life. When you meditate, bring to your mind a symbol or person that represents the problem in your life and hold it or the person in a violet glow of light. You will soon find that ideas come to you about how you can restore harmony to your life and put things right.

When you meditate it is a good idea to put as much ritual into it as possible. Always light a candle and contemplate the little flame as symbolic of the light that is within every heart. For Taureans it is a good idea if you listen to beautiful music before you meditate to lift your Taurean soul and bring your awareness to a spiritual level. It is also a good idea to have something beautiful on your altar such as flowers or a beautiful picture which you can contemplate to further increase your spiritual awareness. Taurus rules the throat, so you may well find it helpful to speak aloud a prayer or sound the great *om*. Singing or chanting a mantra is also useful to Taureans to heighten the feeling of ritual in meditation.

The first meditation with Lehatiel will restore energy to you when you are feeling low and out of sorts. Practice it every time you feel run down and exhausted and you will soon find your energy levels increase and a new confidence and determination to live life to the fullest will come to you.

The second meditation will bring spiritual awareness to your soul and bring harmony to your life and will reveal to you the secrets of your life's purpose. Lehatiel will bring spiritual wisdom to your mind and heart and lead you to follow the spiritual path with a confidence and energy that brings rich rewards. Practice it every day and you will find a deep peace permeates your entire being and new awareness brings insights and revelations to your mind that will lift you to a higher level of spiritual comprehension.

The third meditation with Lehatiel will help sort out problems in your life that you are having difficulty in solving. Lehatiel will bring his harmony and healing to any distress you feel and lead you to make the right choices to resolve the situation.

Meditation to Restore Energy and Bring New Heights of Consciousness

Sit comfortably and prepare yourself for meditation as detailed in the introduction. Before you stands Lehatiel, the angel of the violet ray, radiating a vibrant violet light. This light permeates your whole being, mind, body, and soul and revitalises you. Feel the light as an energy flowing through your limbs and body bring fresh energy to your tired body and mind. Feel yourself aglow with the violet light as it stimulates your inner spirit to new heights of consciousness. You feel able to cope with all your duties in life and a new energy permeates your soul. Hold this feeling for as long as you feel comfortable then bring your awareness back to your actual surroundings. You feel well and refreshed and you know that you can undertake all your responsibilities with a renewed energy. This meditation will also bring a softening of the famous Taurean stubbornness and you will appreciate that sometimes it is better to let go and understand the other person's point of view.

Meditation to Attain Spiritual Awareness

Sit comfortably and prepare for meditation as suggested in the introduction. When you feel ready imagine yourself in a small temple filled with a beautiful violet light. This light emanates from the beautiful angel that stands before you. This is Lehatiel and he holds out his hands in a sign of welcome. From him there comes a ray of pure violet that enfolds you and permeates your entire being, mind, body, and soul. You feel greatly uplifted as the angel imparts his wisdom to you and heals any disharmony there is in your soul. Know that you will reach new heights of consciousness and understanding of spiritual law. The purpose for your life will be made clear, and you will feel a new resolve to follow the spiritual path with renewed energy.

Relax in the harmonising violet light of Lehatiel and let your mind concentrate on this light. All the wisdom of the angel is yours. Contemplate this thought and feel all negativity gently easing away out of your soul. Feel a renewed energy in your physical and mental bodies and know that you can overcome all problems that arise in your life. Through the power of Lehatiel you will bring comfort to those who are distressed and confidence to those who seek help.

Contemplate these thoughts for as long as you feel comfortable then bring your awareness back to your actual surroundings and take some deep breaths. This is a powerful meditation, for Lehatiel is a very powerful angel, and over the next few days you will receive insights into spiritual law that will bring a new meaning to your life. Ideas will also come as to how to deal with problems, so always have a notebook handy to take down notes. This is a valuable meditation to practice in readiness for the meditation with Anael, the angel of Venus, to attain spiritual illumination.

Meditation to Overcome Problems in Your Life

When one has anxieties it is difficult to live your life according to spiritual values, for anxiety itself is a statement that you do not have faith in the angels or in your higher spiritual self. The meditation with Lehatiel, the angel of the violet ray, will help dissolve these anxieties, be they money related or relationship related, or any disaster that has happened in your life. Lehatiel will restore your faith in a higher power and bring you to a place of peace and enable you to see clearly how to deal with the problem in a focused and positive way. Lehatiel will restore harmony to your life and bring a new understanding of the workings of spiritual law.

Make yourself comfortable and warm, and prepare for meditation as detailed in the introduction. Before you stands Lehatiel, radiating a glorious violet light. This light enfolds you and permeates every cell of your being. Imagine a symbol of the problem that causes you anxiety and hold that symbol in the light of Lehatiel.

Know that all will be well and all will work out for the very best for all concerned. If you have money problems, ask Lehatiel for help in this matter and know that a solution will come to you. Feel yourself glowing with the angel's violet light and know that all will be well, for you are guided and looked after every moment of your life. All anxiety and distress gently melts away out of your mind and soul and you feel refreshed and at peace with your life. Hold this feeling for as long as you feel comfortable and then bring your awareness back to your actual surroundings.

Repeat this meditation daily until you feel the problem has worked itself out and you feel that all is well. You will be surprised at what can happen when you ask the angels for help and your faith will be restored in divine guidance. Give thanks to Lehatiel for giving you so much support and help, and also send him your love. You will find your anxiety greatly decreases when you put your trust in angels and Lehatiel will not let you down. Peace will come to your heart and mind, and your life will be much happier when you work with angels and believe in their help and guidance.

Anael, the Angel of Venus

The influence of Venus on Taurus is profound: Taureans are thus concerned with perfecting love, the creative principle throughout life. Anael, the angel of Venus, comes to the Taurean to bring her message of love, the healing balm that rights all wrongs. She brings harmony to the distressed soul. She is the angel of unity, harmony, and beauty, and as we have already seen, beauty and harmony are very close to the Taurean heart. Through the fixed earth sign of Taurus, Venus is associated with money, possessions, comfort, and security, all things that mean much to the Taurean soul. Anael, the angel of Venus, watches over the Taurus personality and brings help to learn the lessons of this sign, lessons that can seem quite hard at times when they are linked to money and security. The lesson of service which we have already covered is very much linked to the ray of Venus, and you will find that great help will come to you when you meditate with this angel.

Anael will bring the understanding that beauty of character is expressed in the ability to balance and moderate the inharmonious elements within the soul. What we think, we become, and Anael will help the Taurean soul gradually to become so steeped in the idea of perfect beauty that this is unconsciously expressed in every action and movement. The more evolved your soul the more by your own strength will you create beauty and perfection in your environment. Anael will bring such elements to your soul and your light will shine forth into the world to bring healing and harmony where there are negative conditions.

Venus is very much associated with the love and wisdom of divine mother and those Taureans who have a strong influence of Venus, either man or woman, have as one of their lessons the creation of love and wisdom through service in every aspect of life. The influence of divine mother brings a caring attitude and a nurturing aspect to the soul, whether male or female, and this wonderful ray can bring great joy to your soul. Anael, the angel of Venus, will help you find practical expressions of love and wisdom, for Taureans are apt to dream and drift, indulging their love of pleasure and gracious living. Anael will support you in your endeavours to bring into reality the harmonising ray of divine mother.

Taurus people are not fighters and yearn for a placid and harmonious existence, but all too often you find yourself at the centre of conflict and you often find yourself drawn into other people's problems. Anael can bring great comfort and wisdom at such times and to meditate with this angel will bring peace and a revelation of the best way forward.

Anael will bring you into direct contact with the love and wisdom of the divine mother and will also open your mind to spiritual truths and help you connect with the divine within yourself. The influence of Venus will bring a search for meaning in life and aspiration to a higher goal than the mere physical. Anael will take you to new heights where you will enjoy spiritual revelation, bringing a new meaning to all aspects of your daily life.

The ray of Anael brings to Taureans the lesson of walking the middle path of balance and harmony. You are learning to find the centre of light and creative power within your own soul and having found it, to remain true to that light. This can be a very difficult lesson for the Taurean, as you don't like conflict of any sort and yearn for peace and comfort both of body and soul. To gain this you are sometimes tempted to evade the issue to obtain peace and do not follow what you know to be the true path. Anael will bring strength and clear thinking at such times and you will find that by following the light within, or what you know to be the truth, peace will indeed come to you.

Taureans often find themselves in the middle of conflict between parties that mean a great deal to them. Not wanting to take sides, you find such circumstances very distressing and long for peace to reign again. It is impossible to take sides and you find yourself caught up in very unsettling situations. The meditation with Anael will bring you wisdom to bring peace and a conclusion to the situation that brings satisfaction to all sides in the matter.

The beauty of Venus will illuminate your soul to bring harmony to your life and those around you, bringing a wonderful healing to negative situations. Let Anael shine her light upon you and bring you spiritual illumination that will answer all your questions and bring a new understanding that your soul has been yearning for.

Meditation to Bring Harmony to a Distressing Situation

Sit comfortably and prepare yourself for your meditation by following the suggestions in the introduction. If you like, you can chant a mantra or sound *om* to further heighten your spiritual awareness.

Imagine standing before you a beautiful angel dressed in golden robes. This is Anael, the angel of Venus, and she comes to you to bring harmony to a distressing situation. Feel the light emanating from her permeating every cell of your being.

In your mind's eye, see the parties involved in the distressing situation also standing in the garden. The light from the angel enfolds them and draws out all negative emotions and thoughts, returning peace and harmony to the distressed soul. Anael brings the opportunity for growth and love to come to the distressed heart and also brings wisdom that creates forgiveness. Anael brings to your heart the knowledge that will bring about reconciliation to the parties involved. Know that all will be well and harmonious and that valuable lessons will be learned through conflict. Anael brings love to your own heart and brings the truth that the divine always brings a positive result out of the negative. Hold this image of the parties enfolded in the light of the angel for as long as you feel comfortable, then bring your awareness back to Anael. Thank her for her help in the matter and know that all will be well. She will bring you wisdom and understanding to deal with any situation that you find yourself in that is inharmonious. You will find that as mediator you will bring harmony back to the parties involved and this will bring the longed for peace back to your life.

Bring your awareness back to your actual surroundings and take a few deep breaths. Do this meditation as often as you feel necessary until you feel the situation has improved and resolved itself. You will find that amazing things happen when you invoke the help of angels.

Meditation to Bring the Ray of Divine Mother to Your Soul

Make yourself comfortable and prepare for meditation using the suggestions contained in the introduction. A beautiful angel stands before you dressed in soft pink robes. This is Anael and she brings to your heart the love of divine mother. The angel shines her light on you and you are enfolded in a golden light that permeates every cell of your being. This light brings wisdom to your soul and spiritual knowledge that brings understanding and a new dimension to your physical life. This is a gentle light, for it brings the qualities of gentleness and the wisdom of the divine mother to your heart and mind. Feel the light of Anael bringing peace and harmony to your soul and know that through your endeavours and with the help of the angels you will find a beautiful truth about your spirit that leads to spiritual illumination. Hold this feeling for as long as it is comfortable. Just hold yourself in the golden light of Anael and know that she is imparting all her wisdom and peace and love to you.

When you feel ready bring your focus back to your actual surroundings and thank Anael for her support and help in your efforts to attain spiritual understanding. This is a lovely and powerful meditation that will lift you above the mundane and bring a wonderful understanding of spiritual truths to your mind. Anael, the angel of Venus, will bring you the courage to implement these truths of love and wisdom in your everyday life, and you will find you are living life in a new dimension. Your heart will be full of the pure joy of living, and you will find that troubles melt away in the most harmonious of ways. True inspiration comes from the spirit within, and Anael will help you realise this truth of your spirit. The love of divine mother will be with you to uplift and encourage when life gets tough and Anael will be with you to bring that ray of divine mother to your spirit.

You will find that this meditation uplifts you to new heights of spiritual consciousness and you will find new meaning in your life. Your true purpose will be revealed to you and that is to bring divine love to your daily life, spreading harmony and peace wherever you go and with all you come into contact with. You will find the true beauty of your soul and will realise that in the eyes of the divine, you are a perfect human being. This may be hard to understand, for you think you have many faults, but the divine knows the truth of your being and knows that faults are just lessons to be learned along the way. Enjoy the true beauty of your soul, and enjoy the peace that trusting in angels brings to your heart.

3
Gemini

Pheniel, the Angel of Transformation

The special angel of Gemini is the angel of transformation, whose name is Pheniel. He is a very beautiful angel, full of wisdom and love. He will guide you on your journey of transformation and bring you to a place of deep peace. Gemini occurs at the time when the earth is transforming itself from spring into summer and there is a great power in the elements that you can attune yourself to. Just as the land is developing into full summer so you can harness this energy through Pheniel to transform yourself into a fully balanced and loving personality at peace with your world.

Transformation is the realisation of who you truly are; a beautiful child of the universe, a shining spirit in the world who can bring love and hope to those so desperately in need. Pheniel will open your awareness to the glory of creation and help you live through the glory of your spirit and bring the love of your spirit into your active life. Transformation is far more than just change, it is the realisation that you are spirit and allowing your inner light to transform the worldly self with a radiance that will bring joy, peace, and divine love in all your dealings.

Gemini is the sign of the twins and Pheniel will bring the realisation that you are a dual personality being—a golden spirit as well as an earthly personality. Pheniel will bring the knowledge that the spirit part of you is very real and not something that is insubstantial or vague. Your spiritual self is as real as your earthly personality and Pheniel will help bring harmony and a balancing of the two parts of you to bring about the wonderful reality of the joy of the spirit that can bring healing to all your earthly ills.

Pheniel brings the awareness that you can attain the state of heaven while still in a physical body. By allowing the transformation of your earthly self, with its fears, doubts, and negative tendencies into the shining spirit of your real or higher self you will bring about a deep change in your personality and hope and positive thinking will replace those negative thoughts and feelings that erode the joy of just being. Pheniel will help you bring about such transformation and will reveal the truth of your real nature. He will support you as you look at what needs transformation in your earthly self, giving you his courage to acknowledge the strength and power of your higher or spiritual self. Transformation is not an easy thing to attain, but with the power and love of Pheniel you will achieve it and begin to live harmoniously and at peace with your world. Love will blossom in your heart and Pheniel will direct you as to how best to use this newfound power. With true love of all creation in your heart you will be able to work miracles and Pheniel will be beside you as you endeavour to work the magic of your spirit to bring healing and hope where there is distress. Transforming yourself into the golden light of your spirit will bring you to the state of pure joy which is heaven while still in an earthly body, but your feet must be placed firmly on the ground in the material world, for it is in incarnation that your experiences lead to that state of heaven. Pheniel will guide you with his love and understanding to truly find the peace and joy of the spirit and bring about the transformation of the earthly base metal to the shining gold of the spirit.

The Gemini personality is a restless one, forever looking for the truth in its various forms, but with the help of Pheniel this restlessness can be brought under control and meditation with Pheniel will still the outer consciousness and allow the spiritual mind to manifest in the personality. This is true transformation and will bring a joy to the heart. With the Gemini ability of communication you will be able to bring the truth of the spirit to other seekers on the path of spiritual knowledge.

Transformation allows the essence of spirit to shine forth in your daily life, and Pheniel will guide you to direct your actions and your thoughts through this shining spirit. Pheniel will bring to your awareness the true nature of your spirit and will reveal to you its power, for it is indeed a great power that can bring healing, hope, and joy to all you come into contact with. Pheniel will heal any discord and negative tendencies in your own nature and bring about a positive healing of that which distresses you in your life. With the power of Pheniel and the power of your own spirit, transformation will occur and you will find that all negative situations and feelings are transformed; hope and joy will come to your heart.

True transformation is the acknowledgement that you are spirit as well as an earthly personality and Pheniel will bring the awareness of this truth to your mind and your heart. He will bring positive thinking to your mind in keeping with the altruistic love you feel in your heart for all creation. Positive thinking is very important if you are to lead a happy life and Pheniel will draw out all that is negative in your personality and make way for the positive thought patterns of your higher self.

The meditation with Pheniel will help bring about this transformation into a true child of the divine. You will become the shining spirit you truly are and divine love will flower in your heart. When this happens you experience a wonderful joy and all the fears and doubts of the earthly mind are dissolved in the knowledge that you are a powerful spirit with the help of the angels with you always. Pheniel will always be with you to lift you up when doubts creep in and will transform your doubts into positive knowledge of the strength of the spirit that can overcome all obstacles.

Meditation to Discover the Strength of Your Spirit

Make yourself comfortable and prepare yourself for meditation as detailed in the introduction. Before you stands a beautiful angel dressed in shining golden robes. This is Pheniel, and he holds out his hands in greeting to you. Take his hands and feel his power and wisdom flowing through you, filling every cell of your being. His love and wisdom empowers your mind and you realise you are spirit and a true child of the divine. Through Pheniel transformation takes place and you feel at one and at peace with all creation. Divine love blooms in your heart centre and you feel the joy of heaven enfolding you. All that is negative within you is held in the golden light of Pheniel and melts away. Love and a positive mindset take the place of all that was negative, and you feel a new positivity and love enveloping you and bringing joy a hundredfold.

Hold these thoughts for as long as you feel comfortable, then bring your awareness back to your actual surroundings. Give thanks to Pheniel for his love and wisdom and the transformation he has brought to your soul. Pheniel will be with you as you go about your daily life to uplift and encourage and remind you that you are a shining spirit. Practice this meditation whenever you feel in need of some joy and wisdom and Pheniel will come to you and bring you inspiration and love.

Tomimiel, the Angel of Positive Thinking

The lesson that Geminians have incarnated to learn is the power of positive thinking. Tomimiel is the angel of positivity and will guide you to achieve positivity in all your thoughts and actions. Thoughts are powerful and create your life. Everything starts with a thought and the outcome of your thinking will depend upon whether your thoughts are negative or positive. Tomimiel will help you ensure that all your thinking is positive and good, and he will bring his love to you to help uplift you when you feel overwhelmed by the worries of everyday.

For Geminians this lesson is to train and control the everyday mind so that it becomes illumined and strengthened by the higher consciousness. Geminians have a restless mind, although that mind is quick and receptive and ready to learn. Meditation with Tomimiel will help you control your thoughts so that your mind becomes still and receptive to the guidance of the higher spiritual mind. When you concentrate on heavenly things, you can receive divine inspiration. Tomimiel will guide you in meditation to think through the higher mind; when you do so, your daily life will be controlled with positive thinking, thereby creating a happy and stress-free life.

The ancient myth about the heavenly twins tell that one was mortal and one was immortal, the immortal one always bringing uplifting, strength, and spiritual enlightenment to the mortal one. This describes very clearly the two aspects of the mind. The lower mind is concerned with everyday living and sorting out the many problems that arise, while the higher mind, part of the immortal soul, is illuminated by the shining light of the spirit. This is the soul lesson that Geminians have come to learn. Tomimiel will help you in your quest and will be with you when the lower mind's fretting and negative thoughts take over. He will help lift you up into the light of the higher mind guided by the spirit, and will still the lower mind so the spirit can shine forth, healing and bringing peace to a troubled soul. Tomimiel will help you bring the lower mind under control so it becomes something like a finely tuned instrument that transmits the harmony and love of the spiritual world to bring hope and peace where there is distress. When the wanderings of the lower mind are in control, the instrument becomes distorted, and negativity and depression can follow. Tomimiel will lift you out of your depression and bring to your heart the joy and perfect love of your spirit, a joy and love you are able to give to others who are in distress. This is the lesson of the Geminian: to so work through the higher mind and develop positive loving thoughts that you instinctively know just the right thing to say to relieve the anguish and distress of your fellow man and bring hope and consolation to the heart of your companion.

The intellect of the Gemini personality is very highly developed and is eager to learn and Tomimiel will guide you on the right path for you. He will be with you always as you endeavour to find the love of the spirit in your heart and with that love bring positive illumination to your daily life. Tomimiel is the angel of hope as well as positive thinking and he will bring you hope that you can master your negative aspects and think with a spiritually illuminated mind. Such positive thinking will transform your everyday life and bring peace and harmony to your own heart and to the hearts of all you come into contact with.

Tomimiel will support you as you learn to control the wanderings of the lower mind and endeavour to think through the light of the higher mind. Meditation with Tomimiel will strengthen and control the lower mind so that it always thinks positively and with the guidance of the spirit. Geminians can all too often become prone to criticism and destructive thinking, but Tomimiel will guide the mind away from such thoughts and help shine the clear light of the spirit upon the lower mind so that it becomes illuminated with the divine intelligence that brings love and a steadfastness back to the heart and lower mind. Meditation with Tomimiel will help you always be positive and see the good in all situations. With Tomimiel as your guide you will always express the love and golden light of the higher spiritual mind, and the meditations with him will train you to still your outer mind so that it is as a mirror reflecting the light and positivity of the higher spiritual self. The meditation with Tomimiel will bring positive thinking to be the normal habit of the lower mind and so make your life more harmonious and happy. Such a state of mind can only bring happiness and joy which you will easily bring to all you come into contact with.

Meditation to Gain a Positive Approach to Life

Meditation is a great way for the restless mind of the Gemini to find peace and stillness. Tomimiel will bring a peace to your soul and soothe the fretting of your everyday mind that worries about all that is happening to you, and imagines all sorts of outcomes to your actions. Tomimiel will illumine your everyday mind with the light of the spirit and bring answers and hope where there is confusion and distress.

Sit comfortably and prepare yourself for meditation as suggested in the introduction. Tomimiel stands before you, a shining angel of gold, holding out his arms to you in a gesture of welcome. He has love for you that you feel stimulating your heart centre. Feel his love permeating every cell of your being and touching your outer mind so that it is stimulated to acknowledge the presence of the higher spiritual mind. From Tomimiel comes a shining golden light and this light irradiates your whole being. You feel greatly at peace and your outer mind is still as it contemplates the message of Tomimiel. This message is that all is well and that the magic and wisdom of your higher mind rules your life to a degree that all works out well and you are happy and relaxed. This magic and wisdom illuminates the lives of all your companions and you bring them the message of Tomimiel with the radiance from your heart.

Reflect on these thoughts and concentrate on the image of the golden Tomimiel for as long as you feel comfortable then bring your awareness back to your actual surroundings. Be at peace. Thank Tomimiel for his love and wisdom that transforms your life.

Practice this meditation every day if you can or as often as possible, for it will greatly assist you to think and behave in a positive manner and you will find your mind doesn't worry as much as it used to. You will find your restless Gemini mind becomes more concentrated on those things that matter and you view your problems with a more hopeful and positive heart. As you become more positive in your attitude towards things you will find your life will become less stressful. Tomimiel will help you deal with problems in a positive way and will bring his wisdom to bear on your thinking and actions. Tomimiel will be beside you with his love to uplift when you feel yourself falling short of your ideal positive self, and he will restore your determination to let the light of your higher spiritual mind illuminate the lower everyday mind.

Ambriel, the Angel of the Yellow Ray

The colour of Gemini is yellow, a warming, positive colour and the angel of the yellow ray is Ambriel, an angel full of wisdom and love. He is with you always and will energise you when you are feeling lethargic and tired and will bring sunshine to your soul when you are feeling depressed. The yellow ray is the ray of wisdom, often known as the ray of the philosopher, and Ambriel will bring you his wisdom when you feel confused.

The Gemini soul is very vulnerable to feelings of lethargy and the meditation with Ambriel will bring a feeling of renewed vigour to you physically and mentally. Gemini is prone to doing two things at once, one of the signs of the twins who always do things in twos, and this can lead to a depletion in energy. Ambriel will shine his yellow golden rays upon you and irradiate every cell of your being with a warm glow that will replenish your energy levels and bring about a feeling of joy and enthusiasm. With Ambriel by your side you will feel that you can accomplish anything. He will bring courage to your soul and a determination to finish that which you have started. With the Geminian ability to do two things at once you can easily wear yourself out, but Ambriel will bring his wisdom to guide you to that which is most important and you will realise what to leave for the moment.

Depression is also something that Geminians are vulnerable to, but the power of the yellow ray through Ambriel will heal this debilitating illness and bring you back to a place of balance and joy. When suffering depression you will find you lose all enthusiasm for life and fall into a lethargic state of non-doing. Ambriel will bring his healing rays of golden yellow to lift you up out of the darkness and fill your soul with the joy of bright sunshine. Ambriel knows your soul and its weaknesses and brings his love to heal you. When depressed, it is not easy to meditate. If you feel in need of Ambriel's golden yellow light but do not feel able to meditate just imagine a beautiful angel dressed in shining yellow robes, full of love for you, standing in front of you radiating his yellow light so that you are filled in mind, body, and soul with his golden yellow rays. You will soon feel uplifted and a warmth will radiate throughout your soul and body as the love of Ambriel shines upon you. Just imagining Ambriel and asking him to heal you will bring all the benefits of his healing power.

Being the heavenly twins, Geminians are often of two minds about something. Faced with two choices, you often fret about what would be the best thing to do. This brings confusion to your life and an anxiety that can lead to a depletion in energy. Ambriel will bring his wisdom to you through the yellow ray so that you can make the right choices for your life. The meditation with Ambriel to decide on which should be your best choice will set your mind at rest and bring about harmony and peace to your soul. Ambriel will help you make a decision as to which path is best for you and will give you the courage to see it through. He will bring a clarity of mind and wisdom to help you make the right choices that will enable you to lead an harmonious life free of anxiety and stress. Ambriel can see the consequences of all choices and knows what is best for you. Be open to his messages and you will find life will be much easier and stress free.

Ambriel, the angel of the yellow ray, is also the angel who will help sort things out when something is going wrong in your life. When problems arise and you can't find a solution call on Ambriel to help you sort the problem and restore harmony to your life. His power will heal all ills that trouble you and will bring a conclusion to problems that seemed insurmountable. His love will right all wrongs and give you clear answers as to what to do to bring about balance and peace in your life. When meditating with Ambriel, hold a symbol of the problem in your mind and see his golden yellow light illuminating it and Ambriel will bring his power to solve the problem.

The first meditation with Ambriel works on your energy levels and any depression that you may be feeling. Use this meditation when you are feeling exhausted or perhaps when you are feeling down, and Ambriel's power and love will bring a quick healing. Practice the meditation whenever needed and you will soon feel full of enthusiasm and energy to accomplish tasks you have set for yourself.

The second meditation with Ambriel is for when you are faced with two or several choices and don't know which way to turn. This is a common occurrence for Geminians and can be easily sorted with the help of Ambriel. He will bring clarity to your mind and help you see what is the best choice for you.

The third meditation with Ambriel is to sort out a problem in your life that is distressing you. When problems won't go away it can be very depleting and it is difficult to see what to do to sort them out. The wisdom and love of Ambriel will be brought to bear on the problem and you will soon see a healing and conclusion to the problem. Practice the meditation every day until you feel the matter has resolved itself.

Meditation to Bring Energy and to Heal Depression

Make yourself comfortable and prepare yourself for meditation as suggested in the introduction. Before you stands a most beautiful angel dressed in yellow robes and radiating a bright yellow light. This is Ambriel and he holds out his hands in greeting to you. He positively radiates love and energy, and you feel his warm yellow light permeating every cell of your being. Feel it replenishing your tired body and uplifting your tired mind. If you suffer from depression feel this radiant yellow light radiating through your mind and soul uplifting and bringing a heavenly joy to your heart. Imagine your depression as a greyness that dwells in your heart and mind and see the beautiful shining yellow light of Ambriel dispersing the greyness and replacing it with bright warm yellow. This yellow ray inspires you and lifts you up above the cares of the everyday world. You feel a new energy and enthusiasm for life and Ambriel gives you all his love and support.

Contemplate these thoughts for as long as you feel comfortable and then bring your awareness back to your actual surroundings. This is a powerful meditation and you should start to feel better very soon. Ambriel will be with you to help you rise above your depression and lethargy and he will bring the joy of sunshine to your heart and mind. With Ambriel by your side you will feel you can achieve anything you put your mind to and he will bring you inspiration and joy and healing to your life.

Meditation to Bring Clarity to the Mind When Facing Two Alternatives

Sit comfortably and prepare yourself for meditation as detailed in the introduction. When you feel ready imagine a perfect yellow rose. Hold this rose and smell its beautiful perfume. Really imagine the perfume as best you can and study the perfect and beautiful form of the rose. Really imagine yourself in the middle of the rose; smell the perfume, feel its soft delicate petals. The rose gradually takes the form of a small temple filled with a beautiful shining yellow light. This light is emanating from a beautiful angel who is standing before you wearing robes of bright yellow. This is Ambriel, and he is holding out his hands towards you in loving greeting.

Ambriel radiates his golden yellow light around you, and you feel it shining throughout your entire body, and irradiating your mind and soul. Feel this lovely light energising every cell of your being. Ambriel brings his wisdom to your dilemma and reveals to you the best course of action to take. Imagine a symbol for each of the two choices that you have and hold them in the light of Ambriel. He will guide you as to the best choice to make and will clear your mind of confusion. Think on each choice and you will get a feeling for the one that is right for you. It will come as a glow in your heart centre as to which is the right choice. Don't worry if this doesn't happen, for you will most certainly feel which is the right choice over the next few days.

Hold yourself in the golden yellow light of Ambriel for as long as you feel comfortable. When you feel ready, bring your awareness back to your actual surroundings. Over the next few days you will feel Ambriel's guidance as to which is the right choice for you, but you may well feel able to make a decision right away. Either way, thank Ambriel for his guidance and help and feel his love for you permeating your entire being.

You can repeat this meditation several times until you feel really sure of the best choice to make. Ambriel's wisdom will guide you and his love will enfold you and will bring you to a place of deep peace and satisfaction.

Meditation to Sort Out Problems in Your Life

Sit either on the floor or in a chair, whichever you find most comfortable, and prepare yourself for meditation as suggested in the introduction. Before you stands a beautiful angel dressed in shining yellow robes. This is Ambriel and he will sort out those problems that worry you in your life. Ambriel radiates a beautiful golden light that fills every cell of your being. He gives you all his love and wisdom and you feel confident that your troubles will be sorted. Visualise a symbol for the problem and ask Ambriel for his help in bringing it to a satisfactory conclusion. Hold the symbol in the golden yellow light of Ambriel and see it dissolving away. If you have more than one problem repeat the process for each. Give Ambriel your love and thanks for helping you through this difficult time and know that all will be well from now on. When you feel ready, bring your attention back to your surroundings.

You should see progress within the next few days. Keep a notebook handy to jot down any ideas that come to you about dealing with the situation. Ambriel's wisdom will flow to you to help you see the situation in a new light. Healing will come to you and you should find the problem easily resolves itself. Repeat the meditation whenever you wish until you feel the problem has been dealt with.

Raphael, the Angel of Mercury

The planet that rules Gemini is Mercury and the angel of Mercury is Raphael, a powerful and loving angel who will bring the wisdom of Mercury to your soul. Mercury represents the developing human awareness of the spiritual aspects of life, and Raphael will bring the light of the divine to your mind, bringing his wisdom to your consciousness. This planet is sometimes known as the bearer of the divine light, and Raphael brings to the aspiring Geminian soul the wisdom and love of that divine light. The influence of Raphael is upon the soul-consciousness which uses the physical brain as an instrument for the impressions it receives from the higher mind or spirit. The planet Mercury brings the realisation that the divine dwells within you, and Raphael will help you access this divine power and bring healing to your life and inspiration where needed.

In mythology, Mercury is known as the winged messenger of the gods. This means that he brings the illumination of the higher, or divine, mind to the lower everyday mind. The angel of Mercury, Raphael, will help you respond to the prompting of the higher mind in your everyday awareness and will help you put into action the divine love that illumination brings. Raphael will bring the power of Mercury to your mind, body, and soul. When the lower mind thinks with the wisdom of the higher mind the Geminian will truly find peace and fulfilment. Raphael will assist you in accessing the wisdom of Mercury and help you put into action the illumination that brings divine love to the heart. Through the power of Raphael you will become a messenger of the divine light that shines in the heart of every living being.

The power of Mercury will bring positive thought to the mind which, as we have seen, is the soul lesson of Gemini. Raphael will help you as you endeavour to harness the power of Mercury in positive thought that can do so much to enrich your everyday life. Mercury symbolises the power of thought and Raphael will help your soul rise into the beautiful world

of spirit and heaven. Gemini is an air sign, very much associated with thought. As we have seen, thoughts make our lives.
What we think, we are. Raphael will bring all his power to
help assist the aspiring Geminian soul to that place of heaven
whilst still on earth. It is possible to reach a state of heaven
whilst in the earthly body and the power of Raphael will
bring the awakening divine love in the heart of the soul to
shine forth and illumine the entire being of that soul. This
will bring a wonderful joy that is difficult to comprehend,
but Raphael will bring the power of Mercury to the soul that
aspires to the heavenly world.

The heavenly twins of Gemini also represent the light
and darkness within the soul and Raphael will help you as
you endeavour to gradually bring these two opposing forces
into complete harmony and balance. The influence of Mercury will lessen the power of the darkness within the soul and
bring the power of the light to illuminate the entire being of
the aspiring soul. Raphael will be with you to help and inspire
as you endeavour to bring about harmony within your being.

Mercury is also the communicator and Geminians have
a very well-developed intellect. Mercury is the planet of the
intellect, and communication is one of the lessons that Geminians have incarnated to learn. Indeed they are very good at
communicating ideas and thoughts and when inspired by the
divine higher mind they become great teachers of the laws
and meanings of the spirit world. Raphael brings his wisdom
to the Geminian soul and brings that soul into absolute harmony on the thought plane in the spirit worlds.

The Mercurial ray is the ray of the student, of the soul who longs for wisdom. Raphael will help you as you aspire to greater and more meaningful goals. The heavenly aspiration of the soul is very close to the heart of all Geminians and Raphael will bring you to a place deep within yourself that blends the harmony of the spirit with the love of the divine. Raphael will help you develop that love at the very heart of your being, for it is this love that brings you to experience the joys of heaven. With your powers of communication you can teach this to others, and Raphael will help you as you endeavour to share your wonderful experience of the love and wisdom of heaven. With wisdom comes knowledge of the laws of the spirit and Raphael will guide you to bring into being these laws in your own life. Love one another is the greatest law of all and Raphael will help you when this at times seems very difficult. All souls are aspiring towards the light but some souls seem to be steeped in darkness. Raphael will help you as you endeavour to bring light into that darkness, and he will help you realise that this needs to be done subtly and without force. If you feel very much that someone you know needs some light to bring them out of the darkness, just hold them in the light and ask Raphael for his help. Raphael will be only too willing to help and will guide and inspire you to communicate the light in words and actions.

Words are powerful and Mercury not only rules human consciousness and thought but also the instrument for its expression: the vocal cords and speech. With Raphael beside you, you will find the words to put into expression the joys of the heavenly world that can be obtained by aspiration while still in an earthly body. The Geminian, on the Mercurial ray, have incarnated to train their minds to be instruments through which the heavenly wisdom can be channelled to humanity. Raphael will help you in this lesson and lead you to be a great teacher of the heavenly light that lies within each soul. Gemini, as a dual sign, also brings the knowledge of using words in a harmful and destructive way but, with Raphael beside you, you will be guided to choose words carefully and constructively and to always show a positive state of mind. Raphael will help you guard your speech and will help you to always speak positively and with thought for the feelings of others. Raphael is indeed a beautiful angel who will bring this beauty to your everyday living and help you rise in spiritual awareness to the very heights of the spiritual world. With Raphael beside you, you can indeed experience the pure joy of the heavenly world and have the ability to express this joy to all you know.

The meditation with Raphael will help to bring your mind under control and into a state of harmony, tranquility, and ready responsiveness to the higher spiritual mind with its wisdom that brings divine love to the heart. Raphael will help you bring harmony where there is conflict and love where there is negative emotions. This power of divine thought is like the magic wand of Mercury which brings peace and stillness to the restless mind and brings love and healing where there is distress.

Meditation to Attain a State of Heaven and Spiritual Awareness

Sit comfortably either in a chair or on the floor and prepare yourself for meditation with Raphael as suggested in the introduction. Before you stands a beautiful golden angel. He holds out his hands to you in greeting. This is Raphael, and he is full of love for you. His radiance enfolds you and permeates every cell of your being. He brings the wisdom of the mercurial ray to your soul and illuminates your mind with divine light. Feel this light flowing throughout your body, bringing a deep peace. Raphael brings harmony and balance to your emotions and brings inspiration to your mind. You are truly a messenger of divine love, and you feel full of love for all living beings and creatures. Your heart centre responds to the light of Raphael and he lifts you up, as on wings, into the heaven world. You experience the state of heaven while still in an earthly body and your consciousness attains illumination of the wisdom of the spirit. Contemplate these thoughts and give your love to Raphael. He will guide you into right speech and action and fill your heart with a love and joy that is beyond comprehension.

Hold these thoughts for as long as you feel able, then bring your awareness back to your actual surroundings. Raphael will be with you as you go about your daily life. He will inspire you and bring you guidance and his love will uplift you when you feel life gets difficult. Raphael will guide you to be a true messenger of the divine, and he will show you how to bring your talents to heal and inspire where there is despair and distress. Savour the feelings of joy that Raphael brings to your heart and know that he is beside you as you aspire to experience heaven on earth.

4
Cancer

Zorial, the Angel of Imagination

The special angel of Cancer is the angel of imagination, known as Zorial. He is a wise and loving angel who knows the flights of imagination that can overtake the Cancer personality. Imagination is a gift from the divine and can be used positively or destructively. It is possible to get into a fearful state with imaginings of the darkest kind and feel that all the plagues of Egypt are about to descend upon you. But Zorial will bring his love and wisdom to bear on your mind and free you from the wildest of the most negative of imaginings. The Cancerian mind can have wild flights of fantasy, but Zorial will bring balance and harmony to your imaginings, help you to use your imagination for good, and bring positive energy to your life.

Imagination is very powerful, and your emotions react to whatever you think. What we think, we become; it is important to imagine yourself as successful and loving because thoughts are powerful and led by our imaginings. Your imagination can make you fearful and full of anxiety by imagining things and outcomes that have not yet happened. Zorial will give you the courage of your spirit to dismiss these negative thoughts and he will replace such harmful imaginings with positive thoughts that will work on your emotions to produce a healthy and peaceful state of mind.

Imagine Zorial as a beautiful shining angel and you will increase his power to help; when you imagine him, you allow him become a reality in your life. The spirit world, or all that is divine, cannot be seen or touched. We need to imagine it and our imagination can make the divine real. All that is spiritual is hidden behind a thick veil but we can feel it and experience its energy and power for good in our lives. Zorial will help you realise the divine and bring to you the ability to make real its goodness and positive power in your life. Imagine and believe in the divine and imagine and believe in the angels and you will make them real and thereby bring their power to your life and enable them to help you and assist you in your endeavours to achieve your goals both of the earthly life and in your spiritual awareness.

Used positively, your imagination can help you create the state of living you most desire. Imagination can transform your life and create peace and abundance. This power is very strong, and Zorial will help you think positively to create the kind of life you want. Imagination can help you aspire to your dreams and make them a reality. With Zorial to give his power to your thoughts, imagine yourself as a pure shining spirit and this energy will manifest itself in your life. Zorial will be with you to help you along the path to believe in that shining spirit as your true self and he will encourage you to bring divine law to operate in your life. Divine law means to love one another and the whole of creation, and to act kindly and sincerely in all you do and towards all you meet. Zorial will bring to your mind the power of the light within. The light within is the spark of the divine that dwells in all creation. The spark of the divine can transform your life and bring about positive change where needed. Zorial will assist you to imagine that light and really believe in it. You will feel this light as a glow in your heart centre. Keep it in your imagination and it will grow to illuminate your entire being and life with light and love.

Poets, artists, and great thinkers use the faculty of imagination, and it can lead all of us to the greatest of creativity. Zorial will help you aspire to be more creative in your daily life and achieve things you never thought possible. With the power of Zorial and the power of imagination, you can achieve anything you wish; Zorial will give you the courage to pursue your dreams. Imagine goodness and love illuminating your life, and you will indeed have a happy and creative life.

Imagination can bring into reality spiritual truths. By imagining the angels around you, you give them substance and a reality that will positively help you in your endeavours to reach your spiritual goals. By imagining the light of the divine within you, you give that light a reality that will shine forth and bring healing not only in your own life but will bring healing to all you know. Through your imagination, you can achieve great heights in your creative and spiritual awareness.

On the other hand, living too much in your imagination can be harmful if taken too far. Zorial will help you bring balance to your imaginings so that you live in the moment and from the heart of your spirit. Meditation with Zorial will help balance your imagination so that it does not overtake your life.

Meditation is all about imagination and using it for good. Imagine the temple or garden and see the angel standing before you. By really believing in your vision, you make it a reality. Zorial can use his magic in your life as you aspire to spiritual enlightenment. Zorial will lead you to use the gift of imagination positively to make yourself a bearer of the light who can bring help and healing to all those in need.

Meditation to Use Your Imagination Wisely and Attain a Sense of Safety and Security

Meditation will come easily to the personality born under the sign of Cancer, as your imagination is well developed. However, that imagination needs balancing, as you tend to live too much in your dreams and find it hard to come down to earth. Zorial will help you use your imagination wisely while keeping your feet firmly on the ground. This meditation with Zorial will help balance your thoughts and bring enlightenment to your mind. Zorial will help make your dreams a reality and bring about a new awareness of your spiritual self.

Sit comfortably on the floor or in a chair, and prepare yourself for meditation as detailed in the introduction. Imagine standing before you a beautiful angel. This is Zorial, dressed in shimmering gold robes. He holds out his hands in welcome to you and you take his hands and feel his power flowing through you. His love touches your heart, and you feel a warm glow at your heart centre. A beautiful golden light radiates from Zorial and enfolds you, bringing a great feeling of peace and joy. Feel the golden rays radiating throughout your body, mind, and soul. Know that the power of Zorial brings balance and steadfastness to your mind. Know that his love surrounds you and that you are safe and secure and have no need to worry about the future. All is well in your life, and with Zorial beside you, you can overcome all problems that arise. Zorial helps you think positively about your life and gives you his strength when you feel anxious or afraid.

Hold these thoughts for as long as you feel able, then bring your awareness back to your actual surroundings. Give your thanks to Zorial for his help and his love, and give him your love in return. Practice this meditation as often as you feel you need to. Over time, you will find that your imaginings are positive and you no longer feel afraid for the future. Zorial will be with you to see things in a different light and will bring his love and joy to your heart. With Zorial, you can achieve anything you wish—his love will bring a new determination to your soul and inspiration to you mind.

Muriel, the Angel of Peace

Cancerians are children of the moon and as such are greatly influenced by its different phases. Sometimes you can be moody and unpredictable but long for peace, which is the very lesson you have been incarnated to learn. Muriel, the angel of peace, will come to you when you are feeling down and emotionally exhausted. Muriel will bring the peace of the divine to your soul for he is a powerful and loving angel. Peace comes to the soul when the spirit and the earthly personality are in harmony and not disturbed by any fears and anxieties. Meditation with Muriel will help you blend the wisdom of your spirit with your earthly personality and bring about positive thinking and equilibrium to the mind and soul.

Muriel will come to you to reveal how to obtain peace; as a water sign, you have a turbulent emotional life. You often fear for the future, not only for yourself but for those you love, and these fears are often unfounded. Muriel will bring peace to your soul and help you realise that you cannot predict the future and that such negative thinking can only do harm. Muriel will help you attune yourself to positive vibrations and to let go of your fears and anxieties.

Peace comes to the soul when you have absolute belief in the goodness and power of the divine. Muriel will help you have trust in the divine and he will be with you to bring about a secure future and help you dismiss your anxieties. With Muriel beside you, you have no need to fear for the future, for he will bring his healing love and protection to your soul and help you cope with any problems that arise. He will bring his peace to your soul and bring his wisdom to you so that all anxieties are dissolved in his love. As a Cancerian you often have to combat fear and depression, particularly fear on behalf of family and loved ones. Muriel will bring comfort and a knowledge that all is in the hands of the divine and that all will be well.

Peace comes to the soul when the spirit rules the head and heart. Muriel will help you realise that positive thinking brings well-being to the earthly personality, and in meditation, this angel will bring about a deep peace of the soul. With Muriel's help, you will learn to listen to the "still, small voice within" and know that all is held in divine care and you have nothing to worry about. Muriel will help you deal with all problems that arise in your life, and such knowledge will bring you to a place of peace within. True peace comes about when you have absolute trust in the divine and know that whatever happens is in the natural course of life. This may sound easier said than done for it is not easy to have trust in the divine when things are going wrong around you. Regular meditation with Muriel will light the spark of the divine within you and this spark will steadily grow into a force that can change your life. Muriel will help you realise that the divine within you is real and powerful, bringing you to a place of deep peace as you let go of all your anxieties and fears. Muriel is beside you to encourage and inspire, and his care is with you always.

Cancerians are very affected by the thoughts of others and especially others' turbulent emotions. They can feel emotionally drained and distressed, as they feel deeply for others. Muriel will bring equilibrium back to your emotions and protect you from the influences of others. That does not mean you will no longer care for those in need; quite the opposite, you care deeply for those less fortunate than yourself. Muriel will help you act out of a strong emotional base and bring positive healing to those in distress.

You sense the emotions of others through your solar plexus chakra, and Muriel will help you to strengthen this centre and keep it protected. Whenever you feel yourself being drawn into the problems and turmoil of others' emotions, seek Muriel's protection. He will give you the wisdom and comforting power to deal with the situation. Imagine his protecting wings about you and feel the deep peace of his love. By actively seeking the help of Muriel, you will soon train yourself to withdraw from the emotional disturbances in your environment and will find you can focus your whole attention on the stillness, strength, and wisdom of your spirit. Muriel will bring his wisdom to your mind and his peace to your heart and protect you from disturbing vibrations. With the help of Muriel you will find you can heal and comfort the disruptive emotions of others and can bring to disturbed souls the peace and love of your spirit.

Meditation to Find True Peace of the Spirit

Make yourself comfortable either in a chair or on the floor and prepare yourself for meditation as detailed in the introduction. You become aware of a glorious angel shimmering in gold robes standing before you. This is Muriel. He holds out his hands in welcome to you. Behind you stands your guardian angel, ready to give you support in your meditation with Muriel.

Take Muriel's hands and feel his energy flowing through you. He brings the realisation that you are one with all creation and the divine, and this brings you great peace. In the stillness of the moment, you feel in harmony with the rhythm of your life. Muriel brings you to a place of deep stillness within your soul. He brings the realisation that the divine is within you and is a very real power that can change your life. This spark of the divine glows brightly at your heart centre and dissolves all your anxieties and fears. Imagine a symbol for each fear and anxiety and see it surrounded in Muriel's light. A great peace descends on you and you feel at one with all life. Muriel radiates his golden light around you and you feel it permeating every cell of your being. The golden light of Muriel brings wisdom to your mind, and you know that all is well in your life. You feel a deep peace at your heart centre, knowing and trusting that the divine power looks after you and your loved ones.

Hold this feeling of deep peace and knowing for as long as you feel comfortable, and then bring your awareness back to your actual surroundings. The deep feeling of peace remains with you and you know that the power of Muriel will keep that peace in your heart and soul. Muriel is beside you for encouragement and protection when you feel yourself slipping back into anxieties and fears. Know that your anxieties and fears are dissolved in the light of the divine within you and that Muriel will keep your mind positive and clear thinking. He brings his power to your soul to uplift and heal all negative thoughts and will strengthen your vulnerable emotions. Muriel will remind you of the power of the divine within you, and you will know that all is well in your life. Practice this meditation as often as you think you need it, and you will find that your fears and anxieties dissolve away. With Muriel beside you, you feel a renewed hope for a better future. You know that you are part of the divine and that you have the strength and power to cope with all problems as they arise.

Sattamiel, the Angel of the Silver Ray

Silver is the colour of Cancer, and the angel of the silver ray is Sattamiel, a very wise and loving angel who will bring his wisdom to your soul. Silver is the colour of sophistication and well suits the Cancerian character. It is also cleansing, sensitive, mysterious, and reflects the light of the moon, the planet of Cancer. Sattamiel knows the Cancerian soul is sensitive, emotional, and very receptive to the thoughts of others. Sattamiel will bring his love and energy to you when you are feeling hurt from the harshness of the outer life. Like a crab, you need a "shell" to protect you from the negative aspects of life; Sattamiel will be that protective shield for you, enfolding you in his love and wisdom and healing all emotional wounds that mar your life. Imagine Sattamiel as a magnificent angel dressed in shining silver robes with wings of silver that enfold you and bring you his protective love. He is with you always and will always be there for you, so when you feel threatened or afraid, just imagine yourself enfolded in his protective silver wings and know that all is well with the world.

Call on Sattamiel when you are feeling depleted in energy, and he will bring his power to your soul to uplift and energise your being. It is difficult to live a fulfilling life when feeling exhausted, and Cancerians often find their energy levels depleted by emotional turmoil, both in themselves and when others around them make demands. Sattamiel will bring his energy to you through his silver ray and will uplift you and bring energy back to your body and mind.

Silver is the colour of sensitivity, and you are shy and do not make friends easily. However, when you do make friends you are constant and devoted. Sattamiel will help you in your relationships and bring his silver magic to work on your soul to counteract your shyness and give you courage and fortitude. All Cancerians have the gift of healing, and you are a great comforter to those in need. Sattamiel will come to you to enhance these gifts and help you as you endeavour to develop them. However, your emotions sometimes get the better of you and you feel hurts very deeply and you tend to hang on to them. Sattamiel will heal these hurts and help you rise above your emotions to a clearer and more peaceful state in which you can develop your talents for healing and comforting. These are indeed great gifts to have, and the Cancer personality has to learn to control those turbulent emotional feelings. Sattamiel will help you seek that place of inner peace where heavenly truth will reveal itself to you. Sattamiel knows your mind and soul, and he brings his power to help you seek that peace of the spirit so your talents can flourish. The meditation with Muriel for inner peace will also help you to find peace within the spirit and enable you to accomplish your endeavours of healing and comforting those in distress.

Silver is a soothing, calming colour and Sattamiel will bring these energies to your soul. Silver is also reflective and Sattamiel will help you to reflect on your life and where you are going. He will bring you his wisdom to see clearly what needs changing in your life and he will bring you the courage to put these changes into practice. Change is not something you relish (you become apprehensive at the thought of it), but with the help of Sattamiel you will face change for the better in whatever area in your life it is needed. Sattamiel will bring you to a place of deep peace and illumination and will bring his wisdom to your mind to better cope with all problems life throws at you.

The first meditation is to bring energy back to you physically and mentally when you are feeling depleted or depressed. Whenever you feel exhausted, meditate with the silver ray of Sattamiel and you will soon find you have the energy to face life again. Similarly, the meditation with Sattamiel will bring you back to a place of joy as you realise that you are one with the divine and all is well in your life. Sattamiel will also heal any hurts you are feeling and be as a protective shell to guard you against life's negative aspects. Practice this meditation whenever you feel run down or hurt in any way and you will soon find that your spirits revive and a sense of deep peace envelops your entire being.

The second meditation with Sattamiel is to develop your healing powers and to help bring peace and harmony to those in distress. With the help of Sattamiel you will become a source of strength and hope to many souls in distress who are drawn to you for help. Sattamiel will bring you the courage to put your talents into operation and will heal any obstacles in your way to develop your healing powers.

The third meditation with Sattamiel is to help you reflect on your life and contemplate a change of direction as he illuminates the way forward. Sattamiel will assist with the cleansing and releasing of mental, physical, and emotional issues and blockages as he guides you to a new future. Sattamiel will also help you sort out any problems you are having in your life. These problems can often arise out of your fear of change but Sattamiel will bring his wisdom to your mind so that you can see a clear way forward.

Meditation to Regain Energy, Combat Depression, and Heal Hurts

Sit comfortably either in a chair or on the floor whichever you find most comfortable. Prepare yourself for meditation with Sattamiel as detailed in the introduction. See standing before you a beautiful angel dressed in sparkling silver robes with silver wings. From him comes a soothing silver light that permeates your body and energises it with its sparkling energy. This angel is Sattamiel and he brings you his love and his wisdom. Feel the silver light flowing through your body giving you a renewed energy and enthusiasm for all aspects of your life. You feel renewed and refreshed with a new strength. If you suffer from depression feel this silver energy of Sattamiel flowing through you bringing you the realisation that you are one with the divine. Feel the sparkling silver light of Sattamiel uplifting your spirits and bringing you to a place of joy, a joy that comes from being at peace and at one with the divine. Sattamiel brings you healing and you respond with joy to his silver ray that brings illumination and wisdom from the divine. Be at peace and know that wellness and happiness are your divine right and that from now on depression will be a thing of the past.

If you are hurt in any way, feel the healing light of Sattamiel enveloping you in his love and wisdom, bringing a sense of well being and forgiveness that heals and uplifts you and brings you to a place of deep peace within. This peace radiates throughout your being and you know that all is well in your life.

Hold the feeling of the silver light of Sattamiel flowing through your body and mind for as long as you feel comfortable then bring your awareness back to your actual surroundings. Practice this meditation as often as you feel it necessary to heal your depression or bring new vigour to your depleted energies. It may take a little time for depression to be healed completely, as it is a stubborn illness, but you should find some relief after the first meditation. If you find yourself slipping into a depressed mood, imagine the silver light of Sattamiel enfolding you and you will be uplifted. Remember the joy you felt in meditation and know that a beautiful healing is taking place within you. You will feel more positive and your life will become more harmonious as the healing of Sattamiel begins to take effect in your life.

Meditation to Develop Your Healing Gifts
Sit comfortably and prepare yourself for meditation as suggested in the introduction. See standing before you the angel Sattamiel dressed in sparkling silver robes. He brings you all his love and support. Feel yourself enfolded in his comforting silver light, a light that permeates every cell of your being. Feel the silver light of Sattamiel penetrating deep

into your soul and know that you have the glorious gift of bringing healing and hope to all who are drawn to you for comfort and strength. Sattamiel brings you the courage to put your gifts into action and you know that your healing powers will help all those in distress. Hold these feelings for as long as you feel comfortable and then bring your awareness back to your actual surroundings.

Ask Sattamiel for guidance on how to use your healing gifts and you will find that you will be drawn to a particular school of healing that is right for you. Sattamiel will be beside you as you use your gifts to give support, and he will inspire you to use your gift wisely and positively.

Meditation to Reflect On Your Life and Bring About Changes Where Needed

Sit comfortably either in a chair or on the floor and prepare yourself for meditation as suggested in the introduction. Imagine before you stands a beautiful angel dressed in silver robes that sparkle and dazzle in the sunlight that streams through the temple windows. This is Sattamiel and he enfolds you in a sparkling silver light. Feel this light permeating every cell of your being and bringing a warm love and joy to your heart. Sattamiel brings you the courage to look at your life and see where change is needed. He brings his wisdom to your soul and a determination to accept change and the strength of will to see through any changes that are necessary. The power of Sattamiel will bring peace to your heart; your life will flow smoothly from now on. Believe these things and know that Sattamiel is beside you to resolve your problems with his love and power. If you have a particular problem that is disturbing you imagine a symbol of that problem and surround it with the silver light of Sattamiel. His healing power will help you resolve all problems in your life and will give you the courage to move forward.

Contemplate these thoughts for as long as you feel able, then bring your awareness back to your actual surroundings. You will find that you become more and more reflective of your life and are able to see clearly where change is needed. Sattamiel's power will work on the problem and restore harmony to your life. His love will bring healing to your heart and a new wisdom to your soul that will bring you a reflective understanding. Know that all will be well and that Sattamiel is beside you to heal the situation and bring you his strength and courage.

Gabriel, the Angel of the Moon

The planet that rules Cancer is the moon, and the angel of the moon is Gabriel, a powerful angel who brings deep love and help to the Cancerian soul. The moon represents the great mother of creation and also represents the death and reincarnation each soul undergoes. The ray of the divine mother brings the feminine aspect of life to the soul whether you are male or female and brings with it the creative force of the feminine spirit. Gabriel will bring to your soul the altruistic love that spreads joy as well as harmony when put into action.

Cancerians respond to the moon's phases and can be moody in accordance with its waxing and waning. Gabriel will bring balance to your moods and even out the influence of the moon's rays you so you can achieve a more balanced way of living. The moon's influence is quite strong on Cancerians and can wreak havoc with emotions, but Gabriel will bring his steadying power to your soul and bring peace to your emotional life.

Gabriel's lunar ray will bring a deep desire to care for and nurture all those who are helpless or in distress, especially the young. You will feel a deep love for life itself and will bring healing and consolation to all who are drawn to you. Whether male or female, the home is very important to you and you will relish its security and comforts. A place of quiet and privacy where you can withdraw to refresh yourself is very important to you, and Gabriel will help you create such a space where you can meditate and contemplate. You need a place of sanctuary where you can withdraw in regular intervals to restore your energy, as the Cancer person is apt to overwork and burnout when caring for others. Indeed you are never happier than when spending your time helping people, but a Cancerian can get very caught up in the emotional lives of others. They need somewhere in both the outer and inner worlds to adjust and recuperate. Gabriel will help you create such a place within and will bring you his healing strength to cope with all that may happen in life.

Gabriel will also bring you to a place of deep peace and unity within where you can find the inner child or spark of the divine. You need to nurture the inner child, something the Cancer personality is perhaps the best of all the sun signs at doing. The strong influence of divine mother and the power of Gabriel will bring illumination to your mind and a deep understanding of spiritual life. Gabriel will bring into harmony your emotions, thoughts, and soul, giving you a revelation of the divine Wisdom that governs all life. When Gabriel helps you rise to a plane of heavenly wisdom through meditation, you will find yourself beyond all fear and conflict, and with his help, you will be able to bring this wisdom into your daily life where you bring comfort and caring to those in need as well as positive and healing change to your own life.

Gabriel is the angel of reflection, and under the moon's influence, he will assist you to look back on your life and where you are going. His energy will help you see where you can improve your life conditions, and he will help you when you seek illumination of the spirit. Gabriel, as the angel of the moon, will enhance your reflective moods as they are essential to the Cancerian soul in healing and bringing comfort to distressing situations. Meditation with Gabriel will lift you above your everyday cares and bring you to a place where spiritual truths are revealed to you. This illumination will bring a renewed energy and understanding of the plight of those in need. Your work in caring for others will have a new momentum and new joy that will uplift your spirit and bring hope and uplifting to those you care for.

Gabriel will bring to your soul a sense of deep peace that has hidden strength beneath the stillness. He will bring a dynamic power to your soul that will help you in your endeavours to help others and lift you up beyond the cares of the everyday. Your great sense of altruistic love will be released from your heart centre and you will find a joy beyond comprehension when you realise the divine power that rests within your soul. Gabriel will bring unity of divine energy to your spirit and reveal to you the power that lies within you, unrealised; a power that can change the world when used under the direction of the divine spirit. Gabriel will bring to your heart the aspiration to live a spiritual life which in action means always working from the spirit within and following the spiritual rules of love, integrity, and truth. Divine illumination happens when your spirit rules your heart and head and you realise the divine joy this brings. Gabriel will bring you to a place of deep peace and happiness, and you will know the wisdom of the angels and divine mother. When you attain spiritual illumination, you know that you are part of the divine and that the power of the divine is within you. This is an amazing realisation, to understand that you have that divine power as a part of you. Gabriel will bring this illumination to your soul and you will have new confidence to accomplish your dreams and overcome your fears and anxieties. Gabriel will lead you to attain this realisation and encourage you to follow your dreams.

Meditation to Bring Spiritual Illumination

Sit comfortably on the floor or in a chair and prepare yourself for meditation as detailed in the introduction. Before you stands a beautiful angel dressed in pearly coloured robes and radiating a soft pearl light. This is Gabriel, and he brings his love and wisdom to you to help you achieve spiritual illumination. The pearl light of Gabriel enfolds you and irradiates every cell of your being. Feel this light flowing through you bringing Gabriel's love and wisdom to your soul. Know that deep within you the light of the divine shines, bringing power and strength and illumination of the spiritual life. Gabriel brings wisdom to your mind and altruistic love to your heart. This is the secret of the divine and it brings a great joy to your soul. Hold this feeling for as long as you feel able, then bring your awareness back to your actual surroundings.

Keep a notebook handy over the next few days to jot down any thoughts that come to you which bring new realisations of the spiritual path. Gabriel will be with you to help you keep a true path of spiritual values and will bring a new vigour to your dreams and aims in life. Tune in to Gabriel whenever you feel confused over a spiritual issue and his wisdom will bring the answer to your mind.

5

Leo

Haniel, the Angel of Joy

The special angel of Leo is Haniel, the angel of joy. Haniel is often depicted as female rather than male and is a powerful and loving archangel who directs people who are looking for fulfilment in their lives to the divine source.

Real joy comes to you when you find oneness with the divine, for lasting joy is rarely found in the circumstances of your life. This joy of the divine comes when you actively seek knowledge of the divine source from where comes all wisdom and love. True joy is found when you actively work from the heart centre, or the mind in the heart. Haniel will show you how to find this mind in the heart and help you direct all your actions from the altruistic love for all creation, which is felt in the heart centre, and she will help you tune in to the wisdom that comes from seeking the divine. Working from the heart centre means letting the feelings of love and forgiveness govern your actions and speech, and Haniel will help you in your endeavours to reach this spiritual awareness. Haniel will help you develop the heart centre and teach you how to use the mind in the heart, for this is one of the lessons that Leos have incarnated to learn. Haniel will bring her love to uplift you and will help you shine the light in your heart centre so that it grows bright and steadfast. This light can bring healing where there is distress, and Haniel will help you use this light for the good of mankind, something that Leos in their higher nature long to do.

Haniel knows the personality of Leos and their sunny, cheerful natures and will bring extra enjoyment to your life. You love life and Haniel will be with you as you radiate this sunny disposition and bring joy to other people. Meditation with Haniel will dissolve your fears and anxieties and bring about a lasting joy that only union with the divine can bring. Haniel will bring you to a place of deep peace within where you will experience union with all creation and experience a great joy that will radiate healing throughout your entire being. Haniel will show you how to bring this healing to other people and also bring to them the joy of awareness of the divine.

Haniel teaches you that joy is your natural state of being when you are free from the impediments of your life that block vitality and reverence for life. Pure joy is the closest you can get to a state of heaven whilst in a physical body, and Haniel will help you realise this joy through her goodness and love. Joy comes in meditation when the heart is free from everyday cares and worries, and Haniel will free you from these conditions and bring you to a state that is limitless and beyond the restrictions of everyday life. Joy is achieved when you can see beyond limitations of every day occurrences in life and behold a vision of divine love. Such a vision will bring to you the knowledge that you are held in the protecting power of the angels and Haniel will bring this vision to your inner senses and help you to reach up to the divine will that oversees your life. Joy is knowing unreservedly that your life is held in the hands of the divine and in the power of the angels, and that all will be well and all problems will be straightened out when you connect to that divine will deep within yourself and let joy flourish in your heart. Haniel will be with you as you reach upwards towards the divine source and seek the wisdom and love of the divine.

Let joy into your life by remembering times when you were most joyful. The presence of Haniel will bring these joyful memories to your mind and help you cherish all that is good in your life. Joy is our birthright, and through the power of Haniel you can experience the joy of the divine first in meditation, and then as this joyful light grows stronger, in your outer everyday life. Such joy will fill your life and uplift those with whom you come into contact. Pure joy brings the power of healing, for it confirms the love of the divine in your heart. Haniel, in meditation, will encourage this healing power to grow so that you become a source of strength and comfort to those in need. No matter what life brings try to keep this divine joy at your heart centre so that each day it becomes stronger. Haniel will be beside you to help you in your endeavours and will be there for you when you feel that joy has deserted you. She will bring divine joy back to your heart and help you to radiate a love for life, warmth, and hope to those around you so that you become a beautiful channel for the divine's healing power. When you feel depleted and beset by doubts and fears Haniel will be beside you to bring you back to a place of peace within the heart of your being and rekindle the divine joy that is rightly your true state of being.

Meditation to Develop Your Heart Center and Bring True Joy to Your Soul

Sit comfortably on the floor or in a chair and prepare yourself for meditation as suggested in the introduction. See standing before you a dazzling angel dressed in flowing golden robes. This is Haniel, and she holds out her hands in greeting to you. Take her hands and feel her power flowing through you. This power touches your heart centre and you feel a warm love for all creation. This love grows stronger as Haniel's power flows through you and you feel a great joy blossoming within you. Feel this joy and know that all is well in your life and that you are looked after and cared for by the angels. Haniel radiates a golden glow that enfolds you and brings you a deep peace. In this peace you find a true joy that transcends all earthly worries. This is your natural state of being, and Haniel will fill you with her love so that your joy will flourish. All is well in your life and you know that Haniel is beside you to stimulate that joy in you that comes from contact with the divine. Hold these thoughts and the feeling of pure joy for as long as you feel comfortable, then bring awareness back to your actual surroundings. Thank Haniel for her love and help in finding divine joy within you.

Regular meditation with Haniel will strengthen the continued feeling of joy within you and you will know that all is well in your life. Haniel will care for you and send you her love, stimulating your heart centre so that joy becomes your natural state of being. It is your birthright to be joyful, and you will find that divine joy will bring you wisdom to deal with the problems in your life. You will view life from a new perspective that is much more positive, and you will attract positive vibrations into your life.

Verchiel, the Angel of Faith

The special lesson Leos have incarnated to learn is one of faith. The angel of faith is Verchiel, who is strong and powerful and watches over the Leo personality. He will guide you to find your faith and bring this faith into action in your daily life.

Faith is far more than just a belief in the divine; it is a trust and confidence in divine power and the angels to look after you and protect you with their love and wisdom. Verchiel will help you as you reach upwards to touch that divine power. Having trust in angels means knowing that all will be well in your life and you have nothing to be afraid of. Verchiel will help you realise these facts and bring them into being as you go about your daily life. Having confidence in the angels will bring joy to your heart as you realise that your fears are ungrounded. Verchiel will guide you as you endeavour to bring the truth of divine power to your heart and he will strengthen your trust in that divine power and lead you to a happier outlook on life. Verchiel will watch over you and help you realise that trust in the divine is an unshakable knowledge that life is good and positive and that we are part of the divine. When life does not go as you would wish and you face anxiety or distress, Verchiel will bring you back to a place of strength within the deepest part of yourself. Trust Verchiel to guide you and know that his love and wisdom is with you to give you strength and the courage to face life's challenges. Have faith that he is with you to keep you safe from your greatest fears and know that he brings you the confidence to trust in divine power to see you through the most difficult of times.

Verchiel will help you realise total confidence in the power of angels and this will bring a true joy to your heart. When you know that all is well in your life and that Verchiel is beside you to help you through the trying times, you will have found your true faith and you will experience a pure joy that will lift you into a state of heaven on earth. The meditation with Verchiel will strengthen your faith in the angels and in the divine power that resides deep within you. Verchiel will help you access this power to bring enlightenment and wisdom to your being. True faith is confidence in the angels and a knowing that they look after you. They never let you down and are with you always to guide and uplift. Verchiel particularly will help you reinforce your experience of faith, which will bring you a deep peace where you know that all is well. Regular meditation with Verchiel will bring you to a place of peace within, for faith in the angels will bring about a positive change in you and positivity attracts positivity. Verchiel will help you dismiss the negative thoughts that can do so much harm; confidence in Verchiel will assist you to be positive in the darkest of times.

Meditation with Verchiel reinforces our connection to him and the knowledge that we are in his care. The power of Verchiel will bring to us the confidence that good will manifest in our lives and whatever unfolds is meant to be and in the hands of the angels. Verchiel will support you as you go about your daily life and will bring to your heart a peace that only trust in the positive power of the angels can bring. Verchiel will renew your faith in the intrinsic goodness of life and in the positive power of the divine, and this realisation will bring a renewed hope to your heart that things will work out for the very best. By strengthening your faith and confidence in Verchiel, you will make it easier for him to help you as he will be working with a positive vibration. Faith in the angels will help you realise that the power of the Universe is loving and good and that with the help of Verchiel you will discover your true focus in life.

It is really difficult to have trust and confidence in the power of the angels when you are going through bad times, but Verchiel will be beside you to guide you into the light and restore your faith. Such times are a real test of your faith in the angels but believing in them and having faith in them will lift you out of the darkness and lead you to a bright and sunny future.

Meditation to Develop Trust and Confidence in Divine Power

Sit comfortably and prepare yourself for meditation as detailed in the introduction. When you feel ready imagine standing before you a beautiful angel clothed in pearly robes and radiating a pearl light. This is Verchiel and he comes to bring you his love and wisdom. Feel his pearly light enfolding you; flooding your body, mind, soul, and every part of your being; feel Verchiel's power bringing you to a state of complete peace. In that stillness, you have complete trust and confidence in the power of Verchiel and the angels to bring harmony and goodness to your life. You know you are protected by Verchiel and you put your complete faith in him to lead you to a bright and positive future. You know that angels bring divine goodness to the world and that they have the power to heal all discontent and distress. Angels have the power to bring harmony and healing to mankind and to bring goodness out of negative situations. Feel Verchiel's love and power radiating through you strengthening your faith and you know that all will be well. Hold these feelings for as long as you feel comfortable then bring your awareness back to your actual surroundings. Thank Verchiel for his love and help, and know that your faith will grow and bring great joy to your being. When you have faith you are radiating positive vibrations and these vibrations will attract positivity into your life.

Practice this meditation every day to strengthen your faith and Verchiel will come to you to bring you his love. This love will wrap you in a protective cocoon and will strengthen your faith in angelic power. You will know that all will be well in your life and that you're guided by Verchiel and the other angels who all watch over you and bring you to a place of deep happiness and truth. This truth is the knowledge that angel power is a reality and Verchiel will bring this truth to your life. You know that your fears and anxieties are unfounded for whatever happens in your life Verchiel is with you to guard you from negative vibrations and bring you out of negative conditions into the light of his love and the power of the divine.

Ariel, the Angel of the Orange Ray

Leo occurs at the high point of summer, when the sunshine brings a vitality and joy to the spirit. Leos reflect this sunshine in their personalities as they are warm, outgoing, and positive people who cheer and encourage their companions. The colour of Leo is orange, the colour of vitality and energy; the angel of the orange ray is Ariel, a kind and powerful angel who guards the Leo and brings a joy to your heart. Orange is a warm and positive colour combining the energy of red and the cheerfulness and vibrancy of yellow. Ariel brings you optimism and strength of character and will lift you up when you are feeling down. He will bring a positive cheerfulness back to your heart and strengthen your ability to cope with difficult problems. Ariel will bring the wisdom of the yellow ray to your thinking so that you can deal with problems in a calm and positive way and will also bring you the energy of the red ray when you are having a bad day.

The orange ray is the ray of love, and because Leos vibrate on that ray, they are working on the altruistic ray of love. Ariel will strengthen the love in your heart that you hold for all creation and will bring to you a deep joy, for when love is in your heart you are joyful. Love is the secret power of life and Ariel will help you attune yourself to this ray and find the love in your heart for all creation. When you love unconditionally joy will come to you, and Ariel will help you to use this altruistic love to draw people to you who are in need. Helping others is something that Leos are drawn to and Ariel will assist you in radiating this love with its healing ray that brings hope and joy where there is distress.

The orange ray is one of energy, for it reflects the vigour of the sun, and when you are feeling depleted in energy meditation with Ariel will bring back energy to your mind and body and fill you with enthusiasm to fulfil your tasks. Leo is a fire sign and the vitality and warm-heartedness that makes you spontaneously generous and outgoing sometimes becomes too strong for the physical body and you become exhausted. Ariel will restore your energy levels with his orange light and bring you to a place of peace and balance. Orange is the colour of optimism and positivity and Leos are very rarely depressed. However, depression can set in when things don't go your way. You are a people person and like to be in company but when you are alone depression can get the better of you. Ariel will bring sunshine into your life at such times and uplift you into the realms of joy, understanding, and acceptance. Ariel will help you accept life's lessons and help you over the difficult times with a strength and hope that only comes from the positive energy of angels.

Ariel watches over you and knows the Leo personality with its enthusiasm that can at times be rather overt. Such enthusiasm that is thwarted can lead to hurts but Ariel will be with you to heal the hurt and lead you to accept life as it is and bring you understanding of karma and the lessons you have incarnated to learn. Ariel will help you radiate kindly warmth, strength, and reassurance to others and your confidence in the angels will draw people to you for strength and guidance.

Being on the orange ray, you are a friendly, warm, and good-natured personality, and Ariel will help you optimise these gifts, for they are indeed gifts. You radiate positive energy and are very determined in your ways, but in a more light-hearted manner than those on the red ray. The mixing of yellow brings wisdom to the heart and mind that helps you see things and people for what they are and brings about an acceptance for life as it is. Ariel will help you understand others and their failings and bring to your soul a patience for others who are not as optimistic or positive as yourself.

Ariel is always there for you when you have problems and will bring his power to help heal and resolve any problems that occur in your life. His power will strengthen you when you feel depleted, and he will bring you positivity when you feel beset by doubts and fears. Sometimes when problems arise in our life we find it difficult to know what to do to resolve the problem, but Ariel will bring his wisdom to your soul and his love to heal the situation. Ariel knows your personality and weaknesses and will help you sort things out for the best for all concerned. When you resolutely open yourself to the power of Ariel you will find yourself strengthened and recharged and ready to face anything that life sends your way. Ariel will radiate his love to you, a love that will quicken your heart centre and bring about healing not only in your own life but a healing that will inspire others who are drawn to your warm nature.

The first meditation with Ariel is to bring energy back to you physically when you are feeling depleted. Ariel will flood your being with his orange light and revitalise you with his love and power. He will strengthen your resolve and will also uplift you when you are feeling down. If you are feeling depressed his warm love will lift you out of dark clouds and bring a new zing to your soul. Ariel will bring healing to depression and bring sunshine back into your soul and you will soon find that you face life with a new joy and enthusiasm. A new optimism will empower you to live your life to the fullest. You will find that you have the strength of character to face all your challenges in life.

The second meditation is to resolve any problems and distressing situations that you have. Ariel will bring his orange light to encourage you and support you when things go wrong. Your cheery nature sends out positive vibrations which makes the power of Ariel easier to manifest. Choose a symbol for the problem and hold it in the light of Ariel and things will soon sort themselves out.

The third meditation with Ariel is to find the altruistic love in your heart centre for all creation. Ariel will show you this love, removing the layers of ego and self that cover it. He will help you let this love shine like a light, drawing companions who are in need of some sunshine in their lives. Helping others in distress is one of the lessons that Leos have incarnated to learn and with the help of Ariel you will be able to fulfil this quest and bring joy to your heart. The love in your heart will attract to you companions who are drawn to your sunny disposition and feel cheered by your company.

Meditation to Revitalize and Heal Depression

When you are feeling depleted in energy or are feeling depressed this meditation with Ariel will soon bring you back to your energetic sunny self. Ariel will flood your being with his radiant orange light and bring sunshine back to your life.

Sit in a chair or on the floor, whichever you find most comfortable. Prepare yourself for meditation as suggested in the introduction. Ariel stands before you and holds out his hands to you. Take his hands and feel his energy flowing through you. Ariel revitalises your tired mind and body. Feel yourself radiated with orange light and feel your energy returning to you. You have a feeling of well-being and you know you can now face all your tasks with renewed energy and light-heartedness.

If feeling depressed, feel this orange light lifting you out of the darkness and flooding you with light and happiness. Feel the power of Ariel flowing through you melting all feelings of depression and anxiety and lifting you up to a place of well-being and happiness and belief in yourself and the angels. You know that angel power is with you to help you out of the darkness and bring you into the light. Ariel brings optimism to your mind and heart and you feel uplifted and inspired to live life to the fullest, devoid of doubt and negative feelings.

Hold these feelings for as long as you feel comfortable then bring your awareness back to your actual surroundings. Thank Ariel for his love and care. Practice this meditation as often as you feel necessary. You should start to feel better almost immediately, as angel power is very potent. Know that Ariel is with you so whenever you feel depleted or falling into depression just imagine the orange light of Ariel flowing throughout your body healing and uplifting you.

Meditation to Solve Any Problems You Have

Sit comfortably either in a chair or on the floor whichever suits you best. Prepare yourself for meditation as detailed in the introduction. Before you stands the most beautiful of angels clothed in radiant orange robes. This is Ariel, and he has come to help you sort out your problems.

Radiating from Ariel is a vibrant orange light that floods your whole being—mind, body, and soul—and you know that you have the power to deal with any problems that arise in your life. Ariel will be beside you to guide and help you, and you know that his power will soothe away any fears and anxieties that you have and will restore harmony to your spirit and affairs in life. Imagine a symbol that represents the problem you are having and hold this symbol in your cupped hands. Ariel shines his light upon the symbol and irradiates it with his orange light. The symbol slowly dissolves away and you are left holding in your hands a beautiful orange six-pointed star. You know that all will be well and that you have nothing to worry about.

Hold this image and these feelings for as long as you feel comfortable then bring your awareness back to your actual surroundings. Practice this meditation every day or as often as you feel necessary until the problem has resolved itself. Know that Ariel is beside you shining his love and wisdom upon you as you go about your daily life. He will be with you to bring encouragement and help as you tackle life's problems. Ariel's power will solve these problems for you and help you lead a fulfilled and happy life.

Meditation to Stimulate the Altruistic Love at Your Heart Center

Sit comfortably and prepare yourself for your meditation as suggested in the introduction. Before you stands Ariel clothed in radiant orange robes and emitting a soft orange light. He holds out his hands in a warm greeting and you feel his power flowing through you. His orange light radiates out from him and enfolds you in its soft glow. Feel Ariel's love flowing throughout your entire being, awakening the love at your heart centre. This love blossoms and floods your whole being, mind, body, and soul. You feel a great joy as altruistic love for all creation becomes a reality for you. Hold this feeling for as long as you feel comfortable, then bring your awareness back to your actual surroundings. Thank Ariel for his love and power that has brought you to the point of great joy and know that the love in your heart will grow to a great healing power within you.

Practice this meditation every day and you will feel your love for all creation growing like a great power within you. This love will bring you wisdom and spiritual insights, for this love is the love of the divine. Ariel will be with you, enfolding you in his love and wisdom. Your life will attract positive energy that will radiate the power of the divine.

Michael, Angel of the Sun

The sun is the planet of Leo, and this is emphasised in the Leo character's sunny disposition. The angel of the sun is the archangel Michael, who is the angel of mental power, spiritual illumination, and spiritual growth. Michael is a powerful yet gentle and loving angel who will help you as you strive upward to reach spiritual illumination.

As the angel of mental power, Michael will help you stay positive in your thoughts and help you eliminate negative thinking. Positive thought will help you attract positive conditions in your life, and Michael will guide you with his wisdom to always be positive and cheerful. Mental power is the ability to create from thought and we all have the choice whether to create for good or for bad. Mind power is what creates our lives. Everything starts with a thought, so it is good to keep your thoughts positive. Michael will guard your thoughts and help you keep them positive, thereby creating a positive and happy life. Michael will help you create good, kindly, and loving thought power to bring goodness into your life, and his wisdom will guide you to use this thought power creatively and for good. You can use your mental powers to send prayers of healing into the world where prayers for good are so badly needed. Michael will guide you and will help your prayers reach their target. He will enable you to use your positive mental power for good in the world and direct it where most needed. The meditation with Michael is a form of silent prayer to send healing into the world; as a Leo you have the faith, trust, and confidence in the angel power that makes such prayer worthwhile.

As a Leo you need to meditate constantly on the sun, the source of all life, warmth, and vitality. Michael will help bring the power of the sun to your soul. Spiritual illumination comes when the light of the divine within is so strong it floods your whole being and brings wisdom and divine love to your heart. In meditation you will visualise the light of the sun and the power of Michael pouring into your heart, strengthening the inner light until it becomes like a great cleansing fountain of divine life and strength, irradiating your whole being. Michael will bring an understanding of spiritual law and spiritual mysteries and his wisdom will guide you to find spiritual illumination. The power of the Sun will shine upon you that you will transcend earthly problems and live your life in a state of peace and happiness. Let the power of Michael cast out all doubts and fears. No matter what life brings to you, Michael will help you overcome all obstacles with a strength that can only come from the divine.

Spiritual illumination brings the realisation that we are all one in the divine, and that divine will rules our lives. Through illumination comes the knowledge that there is nothing to fear, for we are held in the love of angels. Michael will bring this realisation to you and will surround you with his protecting love, a love that is completely nonjudgmental and unconditional.

Spiritual illumination comes to those who actively seek it and Michael will bring you answers where you have questions. Love for all creation is the greatest power you can experience, and Michael will guide you to find this love in your heart. With this love will come wisdom and the light within you will grow steadily until you reach full illumination of the soul. Such illumination will bring answers to all your questions on the spiritual path and will kindle the love at your heart centre so that you radiate life, warmth, and faith to all those around you. Illumination will bring the power of healing to your soul and you will become a fountain of hope to everyone you meet.

The meditation with Michael will daily strengthen the light at your heart centre, a light that will gradually flood your entire being, bringing extreme joy to your heart. Such joy will radiate to all those around you and bring healing where there is distress. Illumination literally means "to see the light" and Michael will bring to you the ability to experience the light within your own life. Such light will bring wisdom to your problems and you will daily grow in strength and joy so that you become a beacon of the divine love that is all healing and all illuminating.

The first meditation with Archangel Michael ensures that your mental power is positive and good, bringing positive conditions into your life. When you are thinking positive thoughts you will create joy and happiness in your life, for positive thoughts create positive conditions. Michael will guide you to eliminate negative thoughts from your mind and lead you to a peaceful and fulfilled life.

The second meditation sends positive mental power into the world to bring healing and understanding where there is conflict and distress. This is very important work on the spiritual path, and Michael will guide your mental power to bring help where it is most needed.

The third meditation with Archangel Michael will bring illumination to your soul. He will help the little light of the divine within you to grow steadily day after day until it illuminates your entire being—mind, body, and soul. Michael will bring wisdom to your thoughts and actions and help you realise that you are one with the divine power that rules the universe. Such a realisation will bring extreme joy to your heart, for you will know that nothing can really harm you—the divine is holding you in its love and power.

Meditation to Bring Positive Mental Power to Your Mind

Sit comfortably on the floor or in a chair and prepare for meditation as suggested in the introduction. Before you stands a beautiful golden angel radiating a glorious golden light, the colour of the sun. He holds out his hands in greeting to you. This is Archangel Michael, the angel of the sun, and he comes to you to bring his wisdom and his love. Feel the powerful golden light that he radiates flowing through your entire being eliminating any negative tendencies and know that Michael will help you keep your thoughts positive and cheerful. Feel his power permeating every cell of your being and feel a wonderful joy as Michael brings his positive energy to your soul. Feel the power of the sunlight warming and illuminating your body and soul and know that all is well in your life. Hold these feelings for as long as you feel comfortable and then bring your awareness back to your actual surroundings. Contemplate these feelings for a few moments and know that Michael will be with you to uplift and inspire you to lead a positive lifestyle. Practice this meditation as often as you feel it is necessary. You will know if you have negative thoughts and feelings and these need to be dealt with. Michael will bring his love and power to help you remain positive so that your mental powers create only good in your life.

Meditation to Send Positive Mental Power into the World for Good

Make yourself comfortable by sitting in a chair or on the floor, and prepare yourself for meditation as suggested in the introduction. Before you stands Archangel Michael dressed in vibrant golden robes radiating a brilliant golden light that enfolds you and permeates every part of your being. Michael has come to give you his love and wisdom and help you send positive mental power into the world where it is badly needed. Feel the light of Michael concentrating on your heart centre and feel your own light responding and growing so that it radiates throughout your entire being. Imagine this light shining out from you and filling the temple, then spreading out into the world. Use your mental powers to imagine this light spreading around the world, bringing hope where there is distress and healing where there is conflict. Michael will direct your light to those places that so need help and this knowledge brings joy to your heart and brings growth to the light within you. Imagine your light spreading out around the world for as long as it feels comfortable then bring your awareness back to your actual surroundings.

Contemplate the work you have just done—work that is so needed in the world—and thank Michael for his help. Practice this meditation as often as you feel able to and know that your work is doing a lot of good in the world. You are a channel for the power of Michael to send healing into the world combined with your own power that grows daily as you practice this meditation.

Meditation to Strengthen the Light Within and Bring Spiritual Illumination

Prepare yourself for meditation as suggested in the introduction. See standing before you a beautiful angel dressed in bright golden robes. This is Archangel Michael and he holds out his hands in greeting.

Michael enfolds you with his golden light and you feel this light flowing through you permeating every cell of your being. Feel his love enfolding you and know that his wisdom is bringing illumination to your soul. Feel the light of Michael connecting with the light at your heart centre and feel your light responding and glowing and growing stronger. This light floods your whole being and you feel yourself full of light. The love of Michael stimulates the love you feel at your heart centre for all creation and you know that his wisdom illuminates your mind. Hold these feelings for as long as comfortable then bring your awareness back to your actual surroundings.

Practice this meditation as often as you wish and you will feel the light at your heart centre, the part of the divine light, grow and flood your entire being. You will feel the love for all creation growing stronger each day and will feel a great joy that only love of the divine can bring. Michael will be with you as you strive upwards towards the light, and his wisdom will guide you in your daily life so that you experience peace and joy as you grow daily in spiritual awareness.

6
Virgo

Cheial, the Angel of Serenity

The special angel of Virgo is Cheial, the angel of serenity, a wise and loving angel who will bring serenity to the Virgo soul. Virgos are apt to worry unnecessarily but Cheial will bring his love and wisdom to heal the Virgo soul and bring about a state of peace to your troubled mind.

Serenity comes to the soul when you live your life under the influence of the higher self, that divine part of you that lies deep within and is at one with the divine will. Serenity is more than tranquility, for it is responding to the highest aspect of your being. Cheial will help you awaken to the spirit of the divine and show you how to live your life by the spiritual principles of love, kindness, and compassion, allowing serenity to become a natural state of your being. Serenity resonates from the deepest spiritual part of you and comes from knowing that the angels guide your life and hold you in their love. Cheial will watch over you when you allow his power and love into your life, and he will bring you to a state of deep calm and knowing that all is well in your life.

Cheial will guide you to find the serenity of your spirit that will bring bliss to your everyday living. Cheial will help you cast out all doubts and fears and will bring to you the knowledge that your life is held in the power of the angels and they will never let you down. Cheial will show you that to place your trust in the divine will bring to your being the serenity of spirit that only trust and confidence in the angels can bring. Trusting and knowing that the love of the divine guides your life will bring a deep peacefulness to your spirit, and Cheial will help you to let go of worries and conflicts.

Placing your trust in Cheial will bring you to a state of serenity and spiritual awareness. Cheial will guide you to experience spiritual knowledge in the deepest part of your soul. Cheial will help you realise that when you allow your will to become one with divine will, serenity will follow. You will release all fears and anxieties, knowing that you are in the right place at the right time and no harm can come to you. Cheial's love will release all distress from your soul and allow a state of serenity to exist in your being, casting out all negative thoughts and helping you to see life from a new perspective. Serenity is confidence in the divine power to rule your life for good, and Cheial will help you awaken this confidence and trust in the divine bringing to your soul a sense of deep peace and contentment from which serenity can flow. Serenity is a radiance of peace and contentedness that brings the knowledge that all is right with your world.

The meditation with Cheial will also bring you to the realisation that you are one with all life. Such knowledge will bring a deep peace to your soul as you experience love for all creation. This love is the greatest love you can have and it will grow steadily as you surrender to the divine, until it becomes an energy within you that floods your whole being. This will bring a true sense of serenity and Cheial will guide you to use this power wisely, for divine love is a power for healing not only of your own life but for everyone you meet as well. Such healing work will bring a sense of serenity to your soul, for you will be responding to the highest calling of the spirit.

Regular meditation with Cheial will steadily strengthen your trust and confidence in the divine and in the power of the angels, and this trust will bring serenity to your soul. Put your fears and anxieties in Cheial's hands and he will dissolve them and replace them with a knowing that all is as it should be in your life. He will gently bring you to a state of awareness of spiritual laws that will help you live your life happily and with confidence. These spiritual laws are to always think positively and to act with kindness and Cheial will help you dismiss negative thoughts from you mind. Cheial will help you surrender your earthly personality to the will of the divine, a surrender that will bring a sense of relief as you let go of worries and distress and put your life in the power of the angels. Cheial will be watching over you and helping you as you reach upwards towards the divine.

Meditation to Bring Deep Peace and Contentment from Which Serenity Can Flow

Sit comfortably and prepare yourself for meditation as detailed in the introduction. Imagine standing before you a beautiful angel dressed in the softest pink robes and radiating a soft pink light. This is Cheial, and he is a loving and kind angel who will help you experience serenity, which is the birthright state of your soul. Feel his love flowing to you and feel this love permeating your entire being, bringing a feeling of deep peace and calm. Cheial brings to your soul the knowledge that you are held in the love of the divine and that all is well in your life. He helps you experience confidence and trust in the divine to make all things right in your life and brings the knowledge that you are one with all creation. Such knowledge brings joy to your heart and the realisation that if you surrender your will to the divine will, serenity will radiate throughout your being. Cheial dissolves all your anxieties and fears and brings the knowledge to your soul that you are one with your creator, the divine will. Allow yourself to feel a deep serenity as you let go of all negative thoughts and anxieties. Know that Cheial will be with you always to help you nurture your serenity and keep you calm and at peace. Your serenity will shine through your personality and touch others with its beauty.

Hold these feelings for as long as you feel comfortable then bring your awareness back to your actual surroundings. Imagine Cheial with you guiding you whenever you feel anxious or at a loss as to what to do and he will bring you answers. At such times renew the feeling you had in meditation of your serenity and enjoy the feeling of deep peace and calm it brings.

Betuliel, the Angel of Commitment

The special lesson Virgos have incarnated to learn is one of commitment; the angel of commitment, Betuliel, will come to you bringing power and love to help you find and experience commitment in your life.

Commitment is a wholehearted response to living life to the fullest. Betuliel will help you understand and respond to all that life has to offer and he will give you the courage to move forwards in life and take every opportunity that comes your way.

Commitment is an affirmation that you will do your best in all things and if on the spiritual path commitment is an affirmation that you will work from your very highest potential. Betuliel will help you to reach up to the divine part of you that is one with the divine. When we do not commit to our lives, we cheat ourselves from knowing who we truly are and deny that we are one with the divine, a child of the divine who can accomplish all we want to in life. Betuliel will bring the knowledge that we do indeed have the power of the divine within us and this power gives us the truth that our true selves are glorious beings capable of achieving great things and bringing all our dreams into reality.

Betuliel will help you listen to the voice of the divine within and pay attention to the message it gives. When we truly commit to live by the highest goals of love and kindness true joy will follow, and Betuliel will be beside you to share in your joy and bring you to a place where wholeness and healing can occur. Commitment brings healing to your soul because it affirms that you are perfect as a child of the divine. Betuliel will help you realise that when you commit to being yourself, you become whole and truly at one with the divine. Betuliel will bring to your soul the courage to commit to all that is happening in your life. He will help you see that all is as it should be and that by committing your full awareness to the conditions of your life you will improve those conditions and grow as a personality.

Some people shy away from commitment, believing that something better will come along if they ignore their life's condition. However, this avoidance and negative attitude only asserts denial of life. Betuliel will help you embrace all that is happening in your life, and you will find that commitment to live life to the fullest will bring about a wonderful healing and opportunities that can only bring a positive change in your circumstances.

On the spiritual path, commitment means striving always to work from the divine love in your heart. Betuliel will help you radiate this love for all creation so that it fills your whole being with a joy that only divine love can bring.

Commitment empowers you and brings about a wholeness of spirit whereby you are working at your highest capacity. Betuliel will help you on the spiritual path to commit to the highest in you and this commitment will bring spiritual awareness and illumination for you have asserted your intention to strive to act from the highest part of yourself. Commitment means service to others or to some spiritual ideal, and Betuliel will be with you as you endeavour to work in the service of others on your chosen pathway. Betuliel will share your joy, for service is one of the highest callings on the spiritual path and Betuliel will guide you as to the best way of service for your particular personality. He will be with you as you work in your chosen field and he will help you bring your divine love to bear on all you do. Commitment will bring you to realise your true self and to live from that truth every day of your life, bringing an untold joy to your heart.

True commitment on the spiritual path brings true wisdom for commitment opens up the higher channels to divine wisdom. Betuliel will guide you to understand spiritual laws and always have the right answers to others who are drawn to you as a guiding light of spiritual awareness.

Once you commit, you open yourself to the guidance of Betuliel, who will bring divine wisdom and divine love to your soul. Betuliel will help you as you strive upwards to the very highest part of your spirit and bring the universe's energy to your soul.

To commit to life means stepping away from fear and having the courage to take on life's challenges. Betuliel will awaken that courage within you and help you live your life joyously and free from anxieties. You will know that all is well and that Betuliel is looking after you.

Meditation for Commitment

Make yourself comfortable and prepare yourself for meditation as suggested in the introduction. Imagine standing before you a beautiful angel radiating a soft golden light. This is Betuliel, and he holds out his hand to you in love and greeting. Take his hands and feel his love and power flowing through you. He enfolds you in his love and brings to your soul the wisdom of the divine. Betuliel brings your soul the courage to say yes to life and commit to always living from the highest spiritual ideals. Betuliel will help you realise that to commit to life means knowing who you truly are—a beautiful and perfect child of the divine. And when you know this, it brings great joy to your heart. Betuliel brings you the knowledge that there is nothing to fear in life and that you are a glorious being capable of achieving great things and realising your dreams once you have committed to living your life to the fullest. Betuliel will help you understand that there is nothing to fear from commitment and that only good and wondrous things can come from such a decision. This brings to your heart a great joy which permeates your whole being and brings the determination for growth and self-discovery. When you commit to being your true self, you can truly commit to others in your life. Betuliel will help you realise these ideals and to give wholeheartedly of your best.

Hold these feelings for as long as you feel able then bring your awareness back to your actual surroundings. Thank Betuliel for his help and love. Know that he will be with you as you reach up to the highest ideals in life and commit wholeheartedly to say no to fear and anxiety, stepping forward into a life of growth and self-realisation. Practice this meditation as often as you feel necessary, and you will feel the light and love at your heart centre grow stronger each time so it floods your whole being and brings about determination to live your life through the power of that light and love.

Hamaliel, Angel of the Blue Ray

Blue is the colour for Virgo, a calming and tranquil energy that reflects the Virgo character. The angel of the blue ray is Hamaliel, a kind and powerful angel who stands guard over Virgos and helps them attain spiritual enlightenment.

Blue is the colour of spiritual devotion and religious study, and Hamaliel will guide you to seek the wisdom of the divine. He will be with you as you seek illumination and will help you realise that such illumination comes from a peaceful spirit. Blue is a very calming colour, and meditation with Hamaliel, the angel of the blue ray, will help the Virgo attain peace and find the true nature of their spirit.

Blue enhances meditation, contemplation, and prayer, and the meditations with Hamaliel are very powerful ones that will bring energy to a tired soul and lift your spirits if you are feeling down. Think of a beautiful sapphire blue sparkling in sunlight and you will have the colour that will bring peace and tranquility to a stressed soul. When you are feeling run down and worn out think of a clear blue sky and let the peace and energy of it enfold you and bring energy back to your soul. Either colour will help energise you, and Hamaliel will enfold you with his love and wisdom and help you find that energy within to deal with life's ups and downs.

Blue is the colour of communication, particularly with the voice, and Hamaliel will help you to always know the right thing to say in any situation. Just imagine him in his beautiful blue robes and he will guide you to use your speech rightly and speak the truth through verbal self-expression. Blue is aligned with the throat chakra, so verbal communication comes easily to you. With Hamaliel's help you use this talent with the wisdom of the divine in communicating spiritual ideals and healing thoughts. The planet of Virgo is Mercury, the planet of communication, and Hamaliel will enhance the power of Mercury and teach you to communicate wisely and with healing wisdom.

Concentrating on the colour blue will help reduce stress and bring about a state of tranquility, and Hamaliel is there for you at times of stress to help you relax and unwind. He will help you find that place of peace within that brings divine wisdom to deal with any problem you have. The meditation with Hamaliel will help you sort out any problems that you are having be it with another person or with money or anything else that troubles you. Hamaliel will bring you inner security and confidence, things Virgo people tend to lack, but Hamaliel will be with you at stressful times to give his support and bring you newfound confidence to deal with difficult situations.

Being on the blue ray, the Virgo personality is one of the helper and the friend in need; Hamaliel will help you in your relationships and friendships which mean a lot to you. You like to build strong, trusting relationships and can feel very hurt when that trust is broken, but Hamaliel will be there for you to heal the pain and restore harmony to the relationship. His wisdom will bring about reconciliation, as Virgos hate distress of any kind (especially in relationships) and tend to blame themselves when anything goes wrong. This is not always the case, and Hamaliel will help you sort out the problem and help you also remain true to yourself.

Blue is also the colour of wisdom of the highest kind, and Hamaliel will bring you his wisdom whenever you ask for it. Wisdom on the spiritual path will help you discern between that which is true and that which is false, for there are many teachings on the spiritual path, not all of them on a positive ray.

One of the lessons that Virgos have incarnated to learn is that of service; to serve in any way brings happiness to the Virgo soul. Service is a high calling, and Virgos have the commitment to serve well and stay with it even when life gets difficult. Hamaliel will be with you to encourage and uplift you when you need his help, and you can call on him to bring steadfastness to your goals. Being on the blue ray of wisdom means that Virgos have the intuition and thoughtfulness to serve wisely, and Hamaliel will strengthen these virtues and give you guidance as you bring into reality your mission of service. This service can be on a larger scale involving many people or on a small scale within the family circle. Whichever path of service you have chosen, Hamaliel will be with you to guide you and bring you inspiration.

The blue ray is the fifth ray, the ray of science, which means the power of thought and prayer on the spiritual path. The power of thought creates good and bad in your life and is one of the truths on the spiritual path that Hamaliel will bring to you. Positive thought will bring good into your life because you are what you think. Hamaliel will help you keep your thoughts positive and so create a happy life. Many people on the spiritual path think that constructively thinking positive thoughts to create good or prosperity in your life is wrong, but the power to create is one of the gifts of the divine. Using our imagination to create good in our lives is using this gift for positive living. Many people live a life of lack and think negatively about life in general and wonder why they are not prosperous or happy. It is not in the order of the divine that we live a life of lack. Life should be harmonious, happy, and prosperous. Hamaliel will help you realise that there is nothing wrong in using the power of the mind to create good in your life, for it is a very real gift of the divine and the angels are only too willing to help you imagine and create prosperity and good. Hamaliel will particularly help the Virgo to create by thought power and the meditation with him will enhance your mental powers to create healing and goodness in your life.

Positive thought is a spiritual truth and one of the things we have all incarnated to learn, as it is a spiritual power that with angelic help can heal not only your own life but also the world. Hamaliel will bring to you the realisation that positive thought is a spiritual scientific practice that needs to be cultivated to achieve illumination and joy. Joy is our birthright as children of the divine and negative thought patterns cannot bring about joy or illumination. Let Hamaliel guide you to achieve positive thought patterns and thereby create a joyful and loving life and to bring healing where there is distress.

Creative thought not only creates good in your own life but can be used to help heal the distress of others and also send healing to areas of conflict in the world. This is a kind of prayer that Hamaliel will guide you to achieve. He will bring extra power to your prayers and guide you to use prayer wisely and for good. Hamaliel will help you with your prayers and teach you to pray for positive good in the world and your life. Prayer is very powerful when used for good and when used in conjunction with angels, and Hamaliel will help you realise the potential for positive prayer in your life. This can be to create prosperity or good relationships, for prayer can create anything positive that you desire to make your life better and happier.

The first meditation with Hamaliel will help you learn how to communicate positive spiritual ideals and your true self to the world. Prayer with Hamaliel is very powerful and will bring results that will surprise you. Hamaliel will enfold you with his power and love to bring about positive conditions in your life through positive thought power, and he will help you deal with problems that are distressing you.

The second meditation is to bring energy back to the tired and depleted personality when you have been overdoing it. Virgos tend to let themselves get exhausted in their service to others, but with the help of Hamaliel and the power of the blue ray you will find yourself flowing with energy. You will find that concentrating on the blue ray will help you on your path of service and Hamaliel will bring divine guidance and wisdom to your soul as you choose the right path for you.

The third meditation with Hamaliel is to bring peace of mind and tranquility when you are feeling stressed. Hamaliel will soothe strained nerves and bring back a feeling of serenity to your soul from where positive thought can illuminate your soul. Feeling anxious or stressed will not create a spiritual life, but Hamaliel's power will eliminate such feelings and bring you back to a state of equilibrium and deep peace. You will know that all is well in your life, for Hamaliel can heal any problems that you have.

The fourth meditation is to learn to use prayer for good in the world and in your life. Hamaliel will bring his immense power to bear on your prayers and you will know that your prayers will bring healing to the world and in your own life.

Meditation to Help You Communicate Your Spiritual Truth and to Bring Positive Thought Patterns to Heal Problems

Make yourself comfortable and prepare yourself for meditation as suggested in the introduction. Before you stands the beautiful angel Hamaliel dressed in sparkling blue robes that are the colour of sapphires. He enfolds you in his love and wisdom. Feel this love and wisdom permeating every cell of your being, bringing a positive outlook on life. Imagine the light of Hamaliel dissolving your negative tendencies and thoughts; affirm to yourself that from now on you will be positive in your outlook. Know that all is well in your life and that you are looked after by Hamaliel and the angels. Hamaliel brings his power to your communicative skills, and you know that you can communicate positively your spiritual beliefs to bring help and healing to others. Nothing can go wrong in your life when you have the love of Hamaliel to guard over you. Give your thanks to him for his help and love, and send him your love in return. Know that all problems will sort themselves out in the light of Hamaliel.

If there is a particular problem that troubles you, imagine a symbol that represents the problem and hold this symbol in Hamaliel's sapphire light. He shines his love and wisdom on problems and you know that all will be well and distressing situations will be healed.

Feel in your solar plexus and your heart centre a joy and certainty that all is well in your life and hold this feeling for as long as you feel comfortable. When you feel ready, bring your attention back to your actual surroundings. You will find that your life becomes more positive and joyful as you practice this meditation with Hamaliel and that problems that seemed insurmountable just melt away. Hamaliel will be with you as you attune yourself to his lovely ray, and you will find that your thoughts easily take on a positive outlook which will make your life happier and stress-free. A regular affirmation such as "all is well in my life" is good to say, for it will affirm your positive attitude to life and bring extra power to Hamaliel's ray that enfolds you.

Meditation to Bring Energy Back to a Depleted Mind and Body

Make yourself comfortable and prepare yourself for meditation as suggested in the introduction. See standing before you a beautiful angel dressed in shimmering blue robes the colour of the sky. This is Hamaliel, and he stands before you holding out his hands in love and greeting. Take his hands and feel his power and energy flowing through you. Imagine the colour blue, the colour of the sky, radiating out from Hamaliel, enfolding you and permeating every cell of your being with energy and enthusiasm. Feel the warmth of the sun on you, energising your tired body and mind, and know that you have the energy to deal with your commitments and to enjoy your life. Feel joy in your heart centre and know that all is well in your life. Know that Hamaliel will guide you as you find your right way of service. Just concentrating on the prayer in the fourth meditation here is a wonderful road of service and Hamaliel will bring his wisdom to your heart as you undertake your service to mankind.

Hold the feelings of energy, enthusiasm, and joy for as long as you feel comfortable all the while imagining the colour of the blue sky enfolding you. When you feel ready, bring your attention back to your actual surroundings. This is a very beautiful and powerful meditation, and you should start to feel better right away. Hamaliel will be with you as you go about your daily life, and whenever you feel tired in mind or body, just imagine Hamaliel radiating the vivid blue of sky, enfolding you and bringing you joy, enthusiasm, and energy. He is with you always and will be ready to help you whenever you need him.

Meditation to Bring Peace and Tranquility to a Stressed Soul

Make yourself comfortable and prepare yourself for meditation as suggested in the introduction. Before you stands

Hamaliel dressed in beautiful sapphire blue-coloured robes that shimmer and sparkle. Feel his love enfolding you and his wisdom bringing enlightenment to your soul.

Hamaliel radiates a deep blue light, the colour of sparkling sapphires, and this light enfolds you, permeating every cell of your being, relieving stress and tension, and bringing a deep peace and tranquility to your soul. Really feel the deep blue ray enfolding you and flowing throughout your being. Hamaliel's love fills your mind, body, and soul, strengthening the deep peace you feel. You know he will bring his healing to stressful situations and there is nothing to worry about, for all is in his hands. Hold this feeling of peace and tranquility for as long as you feel comfortable. Then bring your awareness back to your actual surroundings.

Practice this meditation as often as you feel necessary, knowing that the feelings of peace and tranquility you felt in the meditation will stay with you and help you deal with all situations in your life. Hamaliel will be with you as you go about your daily life, and whenever you find yourself getting stressed over something, just imagine his beautiful ray of light enfolding you, calming your emotions, and filling you with optimism that all will be well.

Meditation to Learn the Power of Prayer

The power of prayer with angels can bring about great improvements in your life and can also bring healing to the world where there is conflict and distress. This meditation with Hamaliel is a powerful one working on the blue ray which is the ray of thought power and prayer. Hamaliel will bring a change for the better in your life and will bring his healing power to heal areas of conflict in the world.

Make yourself comfortable and prepare yourself for meditation as detailed in the introduction. Before you stands a beautiful angel dressed in sapphire-coloured robes. This is Hamaliel and he enfolds you with his love. Feel this love permeating your entire being, awakening within you the power of the divine at your heart centre. Feel this power flooding your whole being bringing a deep peace.

Hamaliel enfolds you with his deep blue ray of love and wisdom, and you feel yourself rising as on wings into a world of light with Hamaliel beside you. You feel a deep joy and love for all creation. Hold this feeling for as long as you feel comfortable then pray to Hamaliel that all will be well in your life. Say silently to yourself: "Oh Hamaliel, let thy wisdom illumine my mind and your love illumine my heart so that I radiate your love and bring goodness into my life. Let my dreams come true and help me be mindful of the spiritual law that brings positivity and prosperity into my life."

To pray for world peace, imagine yourself flooded with the blue light of Hamaliel and feel his love stimulating your heart centre. Feel the love at your heart centre growing stronger as Hamaliel holds you in his love and wisdom and feel this wisdom as a blue light radiating out from you into the world, bringing understanding where there is confusion and fear. Feel the altruistic love at your heart centre also as a sparkling deep blue light, and send it outwards from yourself into the world to bring hope and healing where there is conflict and distress. This silent prayer is very powerful, for Hamaliel is a powerful angel and his blue ray is one of the most powerful. When you feel ready bring your awareness back to your actual surroundings.

Practice this meditation as often as you feel it is necessary. Once or twice a week is a good way to use this meditation and used in conjunction with the meditation on positive thought should bring real change for the better in your life. The silent prayer with Hamaliel sending healing into the world will develop the light, that spark of the divine that dwells deep within you. You will feel yourself growing stronger day by day in your spiritual resolve. The love at your heart centre will expand and illuminate your life. You will experience the joy of heaven and draw seekers on the path who are attracted to the light radiating from you.

Zadkiel, the Angel of Mercury

Like Gemini, Virgo comes under the planet of Mercury, but the angel of Mercury for Virgo is Zadkiel whose name means "righteousness of God." He is a powerful but loving archangel who will help Virgos in their quest to obtain enlightenment and illumination of spiritual laws.

It is under the ray of Mercury that the conscious mind develops and Zadkiel will help you to obtain that perfect union within yourself of the spiritual and the earth personality. Zadkiel will help you realise that the earth personality must come under the control of the spiritual mind, for when this happens, you acquire enlightenment and a great happiness. You will find that things go much more smoothly in your life and positive things start to happen. The spiritual mind is positive and creative, and Mercury governs the mind and its power to bring about good or bad in your life. Like Hamaliel, Zadkiel will help you as you endeavour to keep your thoughts positive, for positive thought power is one of the lessons on the spiritual path. Positive thought brings happiness to the earthly personality and has the power to bring about goodness and healing in your life.

Zadkiel will also bring to the Virgo soul the ability to discriminate between the real and the unreal on the spiritual path and to recognise and strengthen the light which is shining in the darkness of matter. On the spiritual path there are many pitfalls and opportunities for going astray but Zadkiel will bring discernment to the soul and help keep you on the true path of spiritual unfoldment. Zadkiel is a very loving angel and he will bring his love to Virgos and enfold them with his wisdom, bringing about the truth of the inner worlds. This truth will bring hope and joy to the soul, for it will reveal the truth that you are a perfect child of the divine and that with the help of Zadkiel you can learn the inner mysteries of life. This truth brings the revelation that you are held constantly in the love of the divine and that no real harm can come to you for you have the support and help of angels who stand guard over you every moment of your life. Zadkiel in particular guides Virgo souls to find the truth of their beings and brings about the realisation that you are one with all life, a truth that brings both joy and happiness.

Zadkiel will impart divine wisdom to your soul that will bring about enlightenment and illumination, something that Virgos strive for on the spiritual path. Illumination means knowing the truth of your being and the reason for your incarnation and Zadkiel has this knowledge and will impart it to you in meditation. Illumination brings the realisation that the divine is pure love and that to have pure altruistic love in your heart for all creation is the purpose of your life. This can be a very difficult lesson, for there is much to forgive in the world and much to distrust and condemn, but Zadkiel will bring a deep sense of understanding to your soul and will bring his wisdom to your earthly mind to see behind the outer appearances and to see with the eyes of the spiritual mind.

With the power of Hamaliel to bring about positive thought and the power of Zadkiel to bring spiritual wisdom that is understanding altruistic love for all creation, the Virgo is well set for pure spiritual illumination to take place whilst in the earthly body. This is the true purpose of your incarnation, and Zadkiel will help you as you strive to put this true purpose into practical application of prayer and positive thought. Prayer is the secret ingredient in spiritual life that supplies the mind with power to bring relief and hope where there is distress, and love where there is conflict.

True prayer can overcome all ills and bring about a truly wonderful healing in a life where negativity and distress are the reality. True reality is hope and happiness and prosperity that brings a rich and positive lifestyle that truly cares for the whole of humanity. Conflict and distress are dissolved in the light of the divine and Zadkiel will bring his power to your prayers as you pray for good in the world and in your life.

In mythology, Mercury was the messenger of the gods who brought messages to humans from the gods on Olympus. In reality, that means that Zadkiel will bring messages from your higher self or the divine to your earthly self. This can come through feelings of intuition or ideas that pop into your head. When true seekers on the spiritual path asks for help or have questions of a spiritual nature, answers will always come, and Zadkiel will bring these answers as they strive for mastership over their earthly personalities. As you ask for enlightenment, Zadkiel will bring you illumination and you will know your true purpose in this life. Zadkiel will always bring you answers to your questions, and he will bring you messages from the divine that will bring about a realisation of soul consciousness. You will always know when Zadkiel brings you a message, for it will ring true and give you a good feeling in your heart centre.

Mercury symbolises the power of thought, giving the human soul the ability to rise, as on wings, to the heights of heavenly freedom to experience the true joy of heaven whilst on earth. The state of heaven on earth comes to the soul when the higher mind is in full control of the earthly mind and we live from the altruistic love in our hearts. Zadkiel will help bring this wonderful state of heaven to you, and you can achieve it with the effort of prayer and positive thought. Free will lies in the power of creative thought, and Zadkiel will guide you to use your thought powers wisely and for creative good. The first meditation with Zadkiel will help bring messages from the divine and answers to your questions. These answers may not happen right away, but sometimes they do, so keep a notebook handy over the next day or two to jot down ideas and answers that come into your head.

The second meditation with Zadkiel is to bring enlightenment to the soul and the experience of altruistic love at the heart centre. When this happens, you will experience a wondrous joy, for you will know that you are loved, looked after by the divine and the angels, and that nothing really bad can happen to you. Zadkiel will bring about a union between the lower earthly self and the spiritual self that will bring illumination to the mind.

Meditation to Bring Answers on the Spiritual Path

Make yourself comfortable and prepare for meditation as detailed in the introduction. Before you stands a beautiful angel dressed in golden robes holding out his hands to you in warm, loving greeting. This is Zadkiel, and he comes to bring you messages and answers to questions you have on the spiritual path.

Zadkiel enfolds you with his golden light. Just relax and absorb his power and love for a few moments and feel it raising your consciousness to a higher level. If you have any questions for Zadkiel, ask them now silently and he will answer them. The answer may not come right away but will definitely come within a short while. Feel Zadkiel's love enfolding you and permeating your whole being and feel happy and know that all is well in your life. Hold this feeling for as long as you feel comfortable then bring your awareness back to your actual surroundings. Keep a notebook handy over the next few days if answers and ideas come to you as you go about your daily life. Zadkiel will not let you down and will bring answers to all your questions.

Meditation to Attain Spiritual Illumination and Unity Between the Lower and Higher Self

Sit comfortably and prepare yourself for meditation as suggested in the introduction. Before you stands a beautiful angel dressed in golden robes. This is Zadkiel and he enfolds you with his golden light. Feel his love and wisdom flowing through you, bringing a feeling of great joy to your heart. Feel your heart centre respond to his love with a sense of pure joy as you aspire to altruistic love for all creation. With such love comes understanding and wisdom and you know that Zadkiel will bring his wisdom to illuminate your soul. Zadkiel will help you as you strive to bring your earthly mind under the control of the higher spiritual mind. Feel Zadkiel's power permeating every cell of your being bringing a joy to your heart that takes you, as on wings, into the highest state of heaven. Here you experience the deepest joy and understand the meaning of your life. This joy will remain with you after the meditation and the reasons for your life on earth will come to you. Relax in this joy and know that all is well in your life and that all will be well in your life.

Hold these feelings for as long as you feel comfortable then bring your awareness back to your actual surroundings. Practice this meditation as often as you feel necessary to experience the pure joy of your being. You will find that spiritual illumination will come to you, bringing answers and reasons for your life. Zadkiel will be with you as you continue to experience the joy of heaven while in an earthly body and you will find that altruistic love will bring this joy to your heart. The power of divine thought will bring harmony out of conflict and raise the soul into the temple of wisdom where divine truths will become known to you. Illumination will bring about a great healing in your life and you will bring healing to others, bringing hope where there is distress and healing where there is conflict. Enjoy your life and live it positively, for Zadkiel is with you as are all the other angels of your sign. They will bring joy and ultimate wisdom to your soul.

7
Libra

Tzorial, the Angel of Courage

The special angel of Libra is Tzorial, the angel of courage. Wise and loving, he will come to you whenever you need courage to deal with difficult situations. Courage is the ability to face difficulties with a positive heart and mind, and Tzorial will be with you whenever you need him.

It takes courage to live up to our highest spiritual ideals for there are always those who will instil doubt and fear when faced with something they lack. Tzorial will help you keep positive and be the person you truly want to be. Tzorial will bring to you the courage to live your life as you really want and will guide you towards your highest good. Being the person you really are means knowing that you

147

are a perfect child of the divine and that you are a beautiful shining spirit deep within the layers of personality. Tzorial will help you live your life in accordance with these truths and give you the courage to always live up to these ideals whatever the situation in your life.

Tzorial teaches you that no matter what happens, he is there to uplift and care for you. He brings the realisation that no harm can come to you when you put your trust in the divine. You will know real courage when you put your faith in the divine and the angels, and Tzorial will be there for you whenever you need him.

Living life with the courage of our convictions can be difficult; there are always those who think they know better or what is best for us. Tzorial will bring you the ability to stay true to yourself, your inner convictions, and look deep within yourself for the truth of who you really are. Knowing you are a child of the divine will bring immense joy and the courage you need to fulfil your life's ambitions and goals. Tzorial will guide you to find the right path for you and will be beside you as you travel your own special pathway in life. Being yourself can take courage, as there are always detractors—including your inner voice—who tell you that you're being silly or outrageous. Tzorial will give you that courage that overrides the fearful voice of the ego, and he will encourage you to be totally the person you want to be and to live your life to the fullest, experiencing your inner vision and your soul's delight. Once you make the decision and find the courage to be true to your deepest divine self, you will have wholeness in your life.

When you face difficult decisions or situations, Tzorial will be beside you to help you find the courage you need within the depths of your soul. He will help you face such difficult times and stay true to yourself doing the very best you can in whatever the situation, be it illness, difficulties with another person, or financial problems, Tzorial will guide you to realise the supreme courage that is the ability to connect with the divine and know that you are looked after and cared for.

Following your dreams also takes courage, and Tzorial will guide you to fulfil your dreams with steadfastness and resolution. He will encourage you to be true to yourself and follow where your spirit guides you. Tzorial will help you realise your dreams in the most enjoyable ways and guide you to stay determined no matter what obstacles appear in your path. He will guide you as to the best way to deal with them and set you on the path of fulfilment.

Courage is believing in the divine and angels, knowing that they are with you no matter your problems. Tzorial will strengthen your belief and your resolve to do your best in everything that comes up in your life. He will teach you that you are one with the divine and that you have more power than you realise. This power can bring fulfilment of dreams and the ability to be true to yourself in the knowledge that Tzorial is with you to guide and help you. He will help you when you face adversity and guide you to look within yourself for the courage to overcome all the odds. Courage is knowing that Tzorial is there for you when you feel afraid and have to face life's uncertainties. At such times he will support you and help you achieve understanding to overcome all fear and carry out your tasks with the joy of the spirit that belief in the angels can bring. It takes courage to let go of your fears and anxieties and put your trust totally in the angels, but Tzorial will give you that courage and help you dissolve your fears and lead a rewarding and fulfilling life.

Meditation to Bring Courage to Your Heart

Make yourself comfortable and prepare yourself for meditation as suggested in the introduction. Standing before you is a beautiful angel dressed in golden robes that shimmer and sparkle in the sunlight. This is the angel Tzorial, who holds out his hands in greeting. Take his hands and feel his power and light flowing through you. Feel this power dissolving all fears and anxieties and bringing a new courage to your heart. Know that you will be who you want to be and that all will be well in your life. Feel this courage as determination to do your very best in all things and stay true to your innermost self. Feel Tzorial's love for you enfolding you and permeating every cell of your being. From now on you are going to remain true to your highest ideals and live the life you want. Tzorial will be there to bring his support and love.

Hold this feeling for as long as you feel comfortable then bring your attention back to your actual surroundings. If you feel able, practice this meditation every day to really let the power of Tzorial work on your fears and anxieties and bring courage to your heart to live life as you want to live it. Tzorial will be with you to help and uplift you when you need courage, and he will bring you the commitment to live your life free from doubts and misgivings.

Zuriel, the Angel of Harmony

The special lesson Libra people have incarnated to learn is harmony, and Zuriel, the angel of harmony comes to Librans to give his wisdom and help. He is a gentle and loving angel who will guide you to lead a harmonious life. Living in harmony means living with balance in your spiritual awareness. Zuriel will guide you to live in harmony with your innermost being, that spiritual part of you beneath the personality. This means living by the divine truths of love for all creation, integrity, and honesty. One of the soul lessons of the Libran is to learn to be absolutely true and loyal to your own inner light. Zuriel will be with you as you strive to live by these rules and bring harmony to your life.

Libra is the sign of the scales in perfect balance, but this does not translate for the typical Libran who finds harmony and balance difficult to bring into reality. When one puts something on one of the scale pans, it immediately becomes imbalanced, which is what happens to the Libran. Often you overdo things and tire yourself out so you go from periods of extreme activity to inertia as you recuperate. You can also find yourself on an emotional seesaw with emotions swinging up and down like a yo-yo. Zuriel will help bring balance and harmony back to your soul and will stabilise your emotions so that you live your life serenely

The divine part of you needs to be brought into balance with your personality, and Zuriel will help you achieve this by awakening your soul to its divine energy. True harmony comes when you can blend the love and wisdom of the spirit, your true self, with the earthly self. The spirit needs to function in an earthly body for it to flourish and grow. Zuriel will ensure that your spirit rules your mind and heart so that the light of the spirit illuminates your whole being, mind, body, and soul.

Practically speaking, how do you achieve this harmony? Meditation with Zuriel will greatly help to bring about the growth of the light within. Zuriel will speak to you and instruct you as to how to achieve perfect harmony of spirit, heart, and mind. Listen for his words of wisdom. They will come as thoughts that just come into your head. Zuriel will also help you live your daily life by the truth of your spirit. In practical terms this means doing your very best in everything and loving unconditionally and altruistically all of creation and especially those you meet. Zuriel will help you guard your speech so that you always speak kindly and with wisdom.

When harmony is achieved within heart, mind, and spirit, the light within can manifest itself so that your soul becomes filled with the light of the divine and shines forth to heal any negativity and also brings healing to all you come into contact with.

Living in harmony means allowing your talents to flourish and grow, and Zuriel will bring his power to your soul to help you achieve optimum expression of your special gifts. Our talents are gifts from the divine and need to be nurtured if we are to lead happy and harmonious lives, and the Libran especially needs to be aware of the power of the divine light that dwells within, for it helps them use their talents to the best of their ability, bringing untold joy to the heart and wholeness to their souls. By using your special talents, you are bringing into being the reason for your incarnation, and by allowing them to flourish you bring wholeness to your being. Zuriel will help you reach your full potential, and he will help you develop your gifts and talents to bring about unity and balance in your life.

When you have harmony in your being, you will radiate harmony in your life and Zuriel will be beside you to bring encouragement to your soul. He knows your mind and your emotions and will help you bring your emotions under control and in balance with your spirit. Regular meditation with Zuriel will bring to your mind ideas for how to achieve full harmony in your being, as harmony creates harmony and you will find that problems dissolve away and life becomes more enjoyable and happy.

Simply being instead of doing will bring you an inner stillness where you can find harmony. Zuriel will help you find that stillness and from it will radiate the light of your spirit. Just sitting still and letting go of everyday cares and frets will bring you to a place of harmony and allow the power of Zuriel to radiate your soul. He will help you in meditation to find the stillness and calmness that leads to harmony of mind, heart, and soul. Just relax and be at peace with the world and you will hear Zuriel's words of wisdom.

You need to hear your own voice above the noise of the day, and Zuriel will help you hear it. Listen to what that voice has to say, and know that Zuriel guides it along with your spirit. In the stillness, look at your life with the eyes of your spirit and contemplate all that is inharmonious and negative. With Zuriel's help, determine to right this in harmony with positive thinking and right action thereby restoring harmony to your life.

For complete harmony in your life, you need to look after your health. Do you eat nourishing food or do you snack lazily on junk food? This is an area that is quite important when seeking harmony. Zuriel will guide you to be more health conscious in your daily life and will help in your determination to adopt good eating habits. Take time to be with nature for this will bring great rewards not only to your body but also your mind. Walking is good exercise and is also good for stilling the mind and contemplating life's goodness and positive aspects. Zuriel will walk with you and bring his words of wisdom to you as you walk in nature, for walking brings harmony to the mind whereby you can commune with your spirit and with angels.

In the stillness of meditation, Zuriel will bring to you the realisation that you are one with all creation and also one with the divine. This knowledge brings the soul great peace and true harmony to every aspect of your being. When you achieve complete harmony in your life you will experience a great peace and happiness.

Zuriel will also bring harmony to inharmonious situations that bother you. If you have difficulties with someone and you wish to bring harmony to the situation the meditation with Zuriel will help ease out the disharmony and restore peace and happiness to the situation. Just imagine that person or persons surrounded by the light of Zuriel and miracles will happen and harmony will be restored.

Meditation to Obtain the True Harmony of the Spirit

Zuriel will guide you in your endeavours to live harmoniously with your talents, with nature, and with all life. Reflect on these things for a while and know that Zuriel will be with you to encourage and inspire you as you strive to eradicate all that is inharmonious in your life.

Make yourself comfortable and prepare yourself for meditation as detailed in the introduction. Imagine standing before you a beautiful angel dressed in pearly robes that glisten and shine with different pastel colours. This is Zuriel and he enfolds you in his love and wisdom. Feel the power of Zuriel gently flowing through you, bringing a deep sense of harmony and stillness to your soul. Enjoy the feeling of stillness and know that you will now live a life of harmony between spirit and your practical life with Zuriel beside you always to uplift and lead you to a new way of living. The power of Zuriel brings wisdom to your soul and you acknowledge the divine light within you that reveals to you your special talents. These talents will flourish under the direction of Zuriel and will bring untold happiness and fulfilment to your soul. You will experience true harmony in your life for your personality will be under the direction of your higher self, or the divine light within you.

If you wish to bring harmony to a situation imagine the person or persons involved standing before you bathed in the light of Zuriel. Feel the power of Zuriel enfolding you also and know that his wisdom and non-judgemental wisdom bring forgiveness and understanding to the situation. Be at peace and know that all will be well and that Zuriel will be with you as you go about your daily life and try to do your very best in every given situation.

Hold these thoughts for as long as you feel comfortable then bring your awareness back to your actual surroundings. Thank Zuriel for his encouragement and help in this meditation and give him your love as you receive love from him. Practice this meditation as often as you wish, and know that

Zuriel is beside you to help you bring a sense of harmony to your life. It is a wonderful feeling to live in harmony with your spirit, and know that the power of your spirit brings wisdom and healing to your life. Zuriel will bring you his wisdom on how to find harmony between your spirit and your practical life, so keep a notebook handy to jot down ideas, for they will be guidance from him. Zuriel will show you the balance between doing and just being and will reveal to you the harmony that this will bring to your life.

Masniel, the Angel of the Green Ray

Green is the colour of harmony and the angel of the green ray is Masniel, a very wise and loving angel who will guide you to find the wisdom of your soul. Masniel will bring to you the power of growth and renewal which the colour green symbolises. Spiritual growth will bring wisdom to your mind and love to your heart for all creation and this will bring untold joy, for you realise you are one with all creation and part of the divine.

Masniel will help you bring balance between your head and your heart and bring stability to your emotions. When your mind and heart are in balance harmony follows, and Masniel will bring this balance and restore a sense of well-being to your soul. Green is a very relaxing colour that will bring peace and a vision of who you really are—a child of the divine. Masniel will help you find that place of peace within that green symbolises and meditation with Masniel will help you sustain that feeling of peace in your daily life. Peace allows the wisdom of the divine to flourish within you and bring you understanding and realisation of your true being.

Masniel will bring his power to you to help you deal with everyday problems in your life. He is a great healer and will heal any distress or anxieties that you have. Through his power you will find that you are better able to cope with life's ups and downs and true harmony comes to your heart. Masniel will bring harmony to your relationships and help you find solutions to problems that worry you.

Green is the colour of nature, and Librans love nothing better than to walk in nature and find relaxation amid the contemplative greenness. That is why green spaces are so precious and we need to ensure that they remain to bring us joy and relaxation. The green open spaces provide us with a sanctuary from the hassles of everyday living and bring back a sense of well-being to your soul that will refresh and uplift you.

Masniel will bring his wisdom and peace to your soul as you enjoy your walks in nature and will help you gain a vision of where you are going in life. Perhaps you feel you are not going in the right direction and need guidance as to how to change your life around for the better. Masniel will bring his wisdom to your mind and heart and give you insights in how to follow your dreams for the future. Green represents renewal; the renewal every year in nature. Masniel will guide you as you refresh your dreams and teach you to express your true self as you gain wisdom and self-confidence through the creative power of his love. This love is totally unconditional and will enfold you bringing enlightenment to your soul. Masniel will open your heart to the wisdom of the divine and will give you the strength and confidence to follow your dreams and find completeness in life.

The green ray will also bring energy when you are feeling depleted and Masniel will bring his power to you to lift you up and restore your energy levels. Think of the green of nature, the spring green that symbolises new growth and that energy of nature will enfold you and bring you back to a place of harmony and balance. It is not easy to cope with life when feeling exhausted; you cannot function as a complete person when fatigued in mind and body, nor can you keep your vision of who you truly are. But Masniel will bring the power of the green ray to restore your equilibrium and revitalise you so that you feel you are capable of dealing with anything.

Green is a very powerful colour and is an emotionally positive colour bringing to you the ability to love and nurture yourself unconditionally. Loving oneself is the key to harmonious living, for if you don't approve of yourself, you will be living a negative life. Masniel will open you to the power of loving and nurturing yourself. The truth of your being is that you are a perfect child of the universe no matter what faults you think you have. Masniel will bring the understanding that so-called faults are lessons to be learned from which you can move on and lead a positive life. It is through understanding yourself that you can understand others and bring your nurturing qualities to heal and uplift.

Being a combination of blue and yellow, the green ray radiates the optimism and vibrancy of yellow and the emotional calm of blue, inspiring hope and a generosity of spirit not found with other colours. Masniel will bring this hope to your heart and you will find that meditation with Masniel will bring about a positive vision for the future and an energy to follow this vision, bringing about a completeness to your life.

The first meditation with Masniel will restore energy to you mentally, physically, and emotionally, as the green ray is very powerful in this respect. It brings balance between your head and your heart, in itself restoring vitality to depleted feelings. Masniel will bring his power to your soul and restore vibrancy to your being so that you feel able to cope with all aspects of your life.

The second meditation with Masniel will help heal and resolve problems you have, be they with other people, monetary problems, or anything else that causes you anxiety. Masniel will bring you hope, insight, and a resolve to deal with problems with a positive heart. He will bring his wisdom to you to bring understanding of situations and how to deal with them. Imagine a symbol of the problem and enfold it in the green radiance of Masniel and healing will come and bring you back to a state of harmony and peace.

The third meditation with Masniel will bring you the wisdom to love and nurture yourself, bringing about a state of harmony in your being. Masniel will help you realise your dreams and bring to your being an understanding of who you really are—a perfect child of the universe. He will bring you a deep peace that will stay with you after the meditation. From this deep place of peace within, you will be able to follow your vision of how you truly wish to live your life and improve things for the better.

Meditation to Bring Energy Back to a Depleted Soul and Bring Balance Between the Head and the Heart

Make yourself comfortable and prepare yourself for meditation as suggested in the introduction. Imagine standing before you a beautiful angel dressed in robes of spring green. This is Masniel, and he holds out his hands in loving greeting to you. Take his hands and feel his power flow through you as you are enfolded in his love. Feel yourself permeated by the spring green energy of new growth pulsating through your tired body and mind. Feel it revitalising you with a new vibrancy. Masniel enfolds you in his love and energy, and you know that you will have the ability to live your life to the fullest and follow your dreams to completion.

Hold these feelings for as long as you feel comfortable, then bring your awareness back to your actual surroundings. Masniel will be with you to help you utilise your energy in a sensible way and ensure you get enough positive rest. He will be beside you as you go about your daily tasks to uplift and energise with his spring green ray. Whenever you feel down or unable to cope, call on Masniel. He will be beside you to bring vitality to uplift your spirits and enable you to deal with anything that happens in your life. Practice this meditation as often as you wish to help you get on the road to recovery.

Meditation to Help You Deal with Problems By Bringing Hope and Insight

Sit comfortably and make yourself ready for meditation as suggested in the introduction. Imagine standing before you a beautiful angel dressed in shimmering emerald green robes. This is Masniel and he has come to help you with the problems in your life. He enfolds you in a beautiful emerald green ray and you feel his love and power flowing through you and you know that all will be well in your life. Use a symbol of the problem you have and hold it in your hands. See the light of Masniel enfold this symbol and permeate it with his emerald green ray. Know that Masniel will help you sort out the problem and that all problems will dissolve away. Masniel enfolds you in his wisdom, and you know that you will have the power to solve the problem in a positive and calm way.

If the problem is with another person, imagine this person standing before you. Masniel enfolds him/her with his emerald green ray and also enfolds you in his ray. Feel his love and wisdom enfolding the situation. Know that all problems will be solved in a positive and peaceful way and that the relationship will continue in a loving and friendly way. If you want the person out of your life, imagine Masniel stepping between you. He raises his right hand and brings it down between you three times to break the bond that ties you together. Know that the bonds that tie you together are now severed and that Masniel will guard you against any negative aspects the relationship brings. Feel yourself enfolded in the love of Masniel and feel his beautiful emerald green ray permeating every cell of your being. You know all is positive in your life and you will now live your life in a fulfilling and peaceful way. All problems dissolve away and are sorted in a positive and peaceful manner.

Hold these feelings for as long as you feel comfortable then bring your awareness back to your actual surroundings. Thank Masniel for his help and give him your love. Practice this meditation as often as needed until the problem is resolved. Over the next few days you will find that the problem bothering you will miraculously sort itself out in a most positive and peaceful way. All will be well in your life and your life will be restored to equilibrium and happiness. Trust Masniel to help you and his help will come in the most amazing ways. You will feel relieved that all is sorted and peaceful again in your life.

Meditation to Bring Wisdom and Peace to Your Soul

Sit comfortably and make yourself ready for meditation as suggested in the introduction. Imagine standing before you a beautiful angel dressed in shimmering emerald green robes. This is Masniel, and he enfolds you in his green ray of love and wisdom. Feel this emerald green ray permeating every cell of your being, bringing you a deep peace and feeling of happiness.

Masniel grants you the ability to love and nurture yourself and thereby create a happy and fulfilling life. He brings his peace to your soul and you know that you have the power to follow your dreams and bring to reality the vision you have for your life. Masniel gifts you with the knowledge of who you really are; a perfect child of the universe, and this grants you the power to bring into reality your dreams and hopes for your life. You know that you are a powerful being and from now on you will live a peaceful, happy, fulfilling life.

Hold these feelings for as long as you feel comfortable, then bring your attention back to your actual surroundings. Masniel will be with you as you go about your daily life, and the deep feeling of peace you felt in meditation will stay with you. He will direct his power to your soul to help you follow your dreams and lead a joyful and rewarding life. Knowing that you have the power of the divine within you and the help of Masniel will give your dreams extra power and you will find that they very soon come true.

Hasdiel, the Angel of Venus

Librans come under the ray of Venus and the Libran angel of Venus is Hasdiel, a beautiful angel who brings wisdom and power to the Libran soul. The influence of Venus is the perfecting of love in all its aspects but when on the spiritual path this love is the altruistic love for all creation. To reach such an ideal is a heady task, for it takes courage to give love to those who annoy you or anger you. There is much in the world that is negative, and it is difficult to feel love for all mankind when cruelty features so much in the news. But Hasdiel will bring his wisdom to bear on your mind and heart, and he will teach you understanding and integrity.

Venus is concerned with all forms of art and those cultural pursuits associated with the higher mental planes of being. Hasdiel will encourage you to develop your talents and follow your inner wisdom to create a fulfilling and rewarding life. Hasdiel will bring you the courage to change your direction in life if you find your life unrewarding. He will inspire you to develop your dreams and ideas for a better way of living, using your talents that may have lain hidden beneath layers of the personality. Hasdiel will bring to your being the wonderful, creative power of Venus for the special task of those born strongly under Venus's influence is the creation of beauty and harmony in every aspect of life.

Hasdiel is concerned particularly with altruistic love. When you can achieve love for all creation, you will find you experience a joy and happiness never felt before. To feel love for all creation is to have respect for your fellow man and fellow creature and for the whole of nature. Hasdiel will guide you to feel this respect and to demonstrate it in your everyday living. When we feel love for all creation, we are expressing the highest quality of our being and confirming that divine love is our reality. Hasdiel will teach you to express this altruistic love in your life and have respect and love for every soul you come into contact with without judgement or criticism. Such love is a healing balm not only in your own life but in the lives of others.

When you give out love, you will attract love into your life and find that your relationships and friendships flourish with the help of Hasdiel. He will teach you that divine love brings divine wisdom, for you have committed yourself to a life of love and positivity. Wisdom therefore comes naturally to you. You will find you understand more about your fellow humans, and Hasdiel will teach you how to use divine love for healing distressing situations. With divine love in your heart, you can achieve all your dreams, for you will be attracting to yourself positive influences. Hasdiel will be able to come really close to you to help you as you pursue your dreams.

Souls on the ray of Venus are learning to walk the razor edge, the middle path of balance and harmony, and Hasdiel will be with you as you aspire to achieve this ideal. Hasdiel will guide you to find that centre of light and creative power within your deepest being and to be true to that light in all circumstances. This is difficult for Librans, as they like a peaceful life and need to satisfy everyone. Hasdiel will give you the courage of your convictions and teach you integrity to remain true and loyal to the light of love within your soul. You will find that through the power of Hasdiel, you bring healing to negative situations and remain true to the light within you, bringing that light to the souls of all you come into contact with.

This need for balance and harmony of the Libran soul
brings disturbance to the emotions which need to be brought
under the control of the higher mind. Librans can find their
emotions are torn all ways sometimes, which is exhausting
and soul destroying. Hasdiel will bring his healing to your
emotions and help you find that inner balance that will
restore harmony to your soul. Hasdiel will also help you
to bring your emotions under the guidance of your higher
mind, that part of you that is part of the divine will or divine
mind. When this is achieved you will indeed feel at peace and
at one with all creation.

Venus brings to the soul the desire to serve in some way.
Hasdiel will guide you to be in the service of the light that
shines forth from your heart and brings healing and comfort where there is distress. He will bring you confidence in
your abilities to serve the divine light, and you will realise
the truth of your being—you are a beautiful, perfect child of
the divine. With this knowledge comes understanding for all
creation because as you respond to the light within, you recognise that same light in all of humanity and realise that you
are one with every human being. An untold joy will come to
your heart for the meaning of your life becomes clearer to
you. Hasdiel will help you respond to the divine love which
is the essence of the light within you and he will guide you to
use its healing power in the service of humankind.

The first meditation with Hasdiel is for developing your talents, something the Venus ray will bring into being. Hasdiel will bring knowledge and wisdom to your soul and the courage to develop your gifts to the very highest standard. He will also give you the courage to change your life if that is what is needed to realise a contented and happy life.

The second meditation with Hasdiel is to discover and radiate divine love in your heart centre. Hasdiel will help you realise the divine love that dwells deep within you and can bring so much healing to the world. He will guide you to use it wisely, for it is a great power that can heal not only your own life but the lives of all you come into contact with.

Meditation to Develop Your Talents

Make yourself comfortable and prepare yourself for meditation as detailed in the introduction. Imagine standing before a beautiful angel dressed in golden robes that radiate a soft light. This is Hasdiel, and he enfolds you in his love and power. Feel this love and power flowing through you and touching every cell of your being—body, mind, and emotions. Hasdiel helps you realise your special gifts and talents and gives you the courage to utilise them and develop them for a better way of living. Feel Hasdiel's power flowing through you and know that you have the courage to develop your talents and make a better and more fulfilling life for yourself. Hold these feelings for as long as you feel comfortable and then bring your awareness back to your actual surroundings. The power of Hasdiel remains with you to help you create beauty and harmony in your life. Beauty and harmony are what Librans desire most, and Hasdiel will encourage you to develop these aspects of your personality to enable you to live a rewarding and happy life.

Practice this meditation every day until you feel you have reach a positive and joyous conclusion. Keep a notebook handy for ideas will come to you from Hasdiel as to how you can develop your talents, and indeed what your talents actually are. He will guide you and enfold you in his love and power, enabling you to develop your talents to the full.

Meditation to Radiate Divine Love

Make yourself comfortable and prepare yourself for meditation as suggested in the introduction. Imagine standing in front of you a beautiful angel dressed in golden robes. This is Hasdiel and he radiates a golden light that enfolds you and permeates every cell of your being. Feel the love and power of the light flowing through you and feel your heart centre respond with a feeling of great love for all creation. Feel this love at your heart centre radiate throughout your body, mind, and soul and feel it radiate out from you to bring healing to the world. Hasdiel enfolds you with his love and brings his wisdom and understanding to your heart. Hold these feelings for as long as you feel comfortable then bring your awareness back to your actual surroundings.

Practice this meditation every day and you will open yourself to the love of the divine. You will be drawn to ways of service and will bring healing and comfort where there is despair and distress. By radiating divine love, you will attract love and positive things into your life and find that your life becomes more peaceful, rewarding, and joyous.

8
Scorpio

Hetiel, the Angel of Creativity

The special angel of Scorpio is Hetiel, the angel of creativity. Creativity is a gift from the divine, and Hetiel is a wise and loving angel who comes to the sign of the Scorpion to help you discover your creative talents. Creativity is the ability to express ourselves through our endeavours in endless ways and through our experiences in life. Hetiel will bring to you the ability to find your unique expression of your soul and to use it for good and positive challenges in your life. Creativity means we are part of the divine creator, and Hetiel will show you how to use this power for positive change in life where needed.

Hetiel will come to you to teach you to be creative in all aspects of your life. Creativity does not mean solely expressing the creative arts such as painting, music, and dance but Hetiel will show you that you can be creative in all areas of your life. Hetiel will show you the best way to express your spirit that longs to fulfil itself. You are a shining spirit and this spirit can express itself in beauty that can transform your life. When we express our true creativity we are making a link to the great creator and our spirits soar with delight at the opportunity to express itself in all its beauty, power, and good. Creativity is the greatest gift we have, for it confirms that we are a child of the divine with all the power and joy along with it. Creativity is the energy that gives form to life, and Hetiel will show the Scorpio soul how to sing of the love and divine power of the great creator and bring joy and fulfilment to your life.

Hetiel will bring to the Scorpio soul the ability to use creative gifts and talents that may lie hidden under the personality that strives to deal with the challenges of life. By opening up to your creativity, you open channels to the divine and Hetiel will bring his power to your soul to help you express yourself in the very highest and best way you can. Find out what makes you feel joy and Hetiel will help you develop it and bring a healing balm to your life. Whatever gifts and talents lay unknown within you, Hetiel will help you discover them and he will help you become a fulfilled and complete individual, for when we express our full creative talents we become whole and complete as a person.

Creativity transforms the old into the new and whatever is happening in your life that you do not like you can change it for the better when you express your complete beauty and positivity that are part of the divine. Hetiel will be with you at times of distress and will show you how to find joy and to express that joy in ways that bring healing and conclusion to problems in your life. When you are expressing your creativity, Hetiel will be with you to enhance and inspire you to positive thought and action. Positive thought is an aspect of creativity for the mind. It is very powerful and creates with thought every waking hour. Hetiel will teach you how to use creative thought for good in your life, for every thought is creative and creates either good or negative things in your life.

It is the purpose of our lives to be creative, but all too often life's challenges hide our creative talents and we stumble along through life never really becoming the person we are meant to be. Hetiel will show you the beauty of your spirit and will reveal to you the great power you have within you that is part of the divine creator. With Hetiel, you can find a few moments of peace from the round of daily tasks to tune into the creative mind and find your own creativity. Use these powers for good in your life and you will find yourself living a life of joy and untold happiness you never thought possible. Hetiel will show you how to manifest the divine power of creativity through your soul and create the life you want to live through the power of your mind. The mind is the instrument through which creativity can flourish and when used for positive good can transform and regenerate your life. Hetiel will teach you how to use your mind to inspire and stimulate the divine part of you and will reveal to you how creative energy gives life form. All things in life start with a thought, and Hetiel will show you how to use your mind to bring joy and fulfilment to your life you never thought possible. If you think mainly negative thoughts, you will have a negative life, but Hetiel will reveal to you how you can change to positive thought patterns and turn your life around. If you find it difficult to think positively try the meditation with Tomimiel, the Taurus angel of positive thought, to really get yourself thinking positively. Positive thought creates a happy, well balanced life, for it is straight from the creative source.

The meditation with Hetiel will stimulate that part of you that is part of the creative will and will help you use this remarkable gift to enhance your life and inspire you to great endeavours. You will find your life becomes more fulfilling and happier, for you will be living from your creative centre which will create a positive and stimulating life.

Meditation to Be Creative in All Areas of Your Life
Sit comfortably and make yourself ready for meditation using the suggestions in the introduction. Imagine standing in front of you a beautiful angel dressed in golden robes, radiating a soft golden light. This is Hetiel, the angel of creativity, and he will bring to you his love and wisdom

to help you live a happy and creative life. He enfolds you in golden light that permeates every cell of your being. Feel this light flowing through your entire being—mind, body, and soul—stimulating your creative potential and focusing on your many talents and abilities. Hetiel's love melts away any negative thought patterns and replaces them with positive energy that will create a happy and fulfilling life for you. Know that all will be well in your life and you can look forward to a joyous and creative life.

Hold the feeling of Hetiel's light permeating your being for as long as it feels comfortable, then bring your awareness back to your actual surroundings. Hetiel will be beside you as you endeavour to create the life you want with the power of your mind. Your creative talents will be stimulated by the love of Hetiel, who will enfold you in his golden light and help you realise your special and unique gifts that will transform your life. Creativity is a gift from the divine, and Hetiel will bring to you his special love to help you realise that you are a creative being capable of changing your life for the better.

Barbiel, the Angel of Compassion

The special lesson that Scorpios have incarnated to learn is one of compassion. The angel of compassion is Barbiel, a kind and loving angel who will bring his wisdom to the Scorpio soul. Compassion is having an empathy with others and understanding their problems and distress. It is appreciating the uniqueness and divinity of each individual and treating each person you meet with kindness and thought-fulness whatever the outward appearances of that person.

Barbiel brings inner strength to live your life as a divine child of God with a peaceful heart and loving kindness whatever the situation. Barbiel helps us appreciate each other and regard all we meet as equals in the light of the divine. Compassion brings the need in Scorpios for service of some kind to ease the suffering of others, and Barbiel will bring wisdom to the Scorpio as to how best to do this using the Scorpio's special gifts.

Compassion brings the desire to do something in the world to ease the suffering of others, whether for human beings or animals and wildlife; there is much in the world that needs healing, and the Scorpio personality is well-suited to leading the way in helping others and bringing about a healing of suffering.

Our compassion is a reflection of the compassion and mercy of God, and Barbiel will bring to your soul the wisdom and caring of the divine. Compassion is about caring; caring how others are feeling and always being positive no matter what the situation. A positive attitude can do wonders to lift the spirits of another who is feeling down, and Barbiel will bring to your soul the ability to bring healing to distress and to bring a truly caring attitude to your everyday dealings.

Compassion opens the heart centre, and Barbiel will bring to your soul the love of the divine and support as you experience the love at your heart centre for all humanity growing and radiating throughout your being, bringing a deep joy and peace. When one feels a true altruistic love for all creation, one feels a deep joy. It is affirming that you are one with the creator and that all have the divine spark within them. The stimulation of the heart centre is the true lesson for all on the spiritual path, and Barbiel will inspire you to learn compassion and act from the love in your heart. When one feels altruistic love for all creation, divine wisdom follows, for you are affirming that negative stimulus does not exist in you. Divine wisdom comes to those who truly believe in the divine power. This may sound like a very high ideal to attain, but Barbiel will inspire you to reach up to the highest level of your being and remain positive whatever the situation.

Compassion needs to be learned wisely, for there is much in the world to feel upset about and it can drag us down. Barbiel will help you keep your emotions positive and feel compassion for all involved no matter what their outward actions. All are part of the divine no matter what they choose to convey and those that display negative tendencies and project a cruel manner are perhaps in need most of our compassion, for compassion brings divine wisdom which teaches the laws of karma. Barbiel will always be beside you to help you keep your feelings positive and not get involved in negative emotions.

With Barbiel by your side, you will lead a happy and fulfilling life, for he will guide you to service and altruistic love that will bring a joy to your heart and divine wisdom to your mind. With divine wisdom comes illumination and you will realise that you are one with every living creature on earth. This will help you realise your true place in the world, as a healer and inspirer of souls less fortunate than yourself. Barbiel will be beside you to uplift and inspire you when you feel limited and unworthy of the ideals you have set yourself.

Meditation to Learn the True Meaning of Compassion

Make yourself comfortable and prepare yourself for meditation as suggested in the introduction. Imagine standing before you a beautiful angel dressed in soft pearl-coloured robes. This is Barbiel, and he radiates a pearl light that enfolds you and permeates every cell of your being. Feel his love and power filling every part of you, your emotional body, your mind, and soul. Feel the power of Barbiel enfolding you and flowing through you. This power and love awakens your heart centre and you feel a wonderful love for all creation. Feel the wisdom of Barbiel stimulating your higher mind bringing illumination and knowledge and know that through this you will develop your compassion for all God's creatures. Hold these feelings for as long as you feel comfortable then bring your awareness back to your actual surroundings.

Barbiel will be beside you as you seek your true place in the world and will uplift you and give you courage as you endeavour to keep to the high ideals you have set yourself. Practice this meditation every day until you feel your work with Barbiel has reached a positive conclusion. Know that his wisdom is yours to access whenever the need arises. Imagine him in his pearly robes beside you and ask for his advice. He is a loving angel and will be only too pleased to help you as you reach up to that highest part of your being.

Acrabiel, the Angel of the Indigo Ray

Scorpios are working on the indigo ray, and the angel of this ray is Acrabiel, a wise and loving angel who will bring peace and beauty to the Scorpio soul. The indigo ray is the ray of the mystic, which means that Scorpios like to understand the deeper meaning of spiritual laws and what's underneath the outwards appearance of things. You are very intuitive, and Acrabiel will help you develop your intuition so that it works positively for you. The indigo ray helps open the third eye, and Acrabiel will assist you in deeper meditation, which Scorpios are very adept at. The indigo ray is very much the ray of the new age and Scorpios are very attuned to the mystical vibrations of the present times. Acrabiel will help you tune into these vibrations and help you open your heart centre to the light of the divine. He will assist you as you reach upward to your higher self and he will help you realise your true potential on the spiritual path.

The indigo ray is also the ray of wisdom, and Acrabiel will help you relate to this wisdom of the spirit as you search for meaning in your life. This is something very important to Scorpios, who search for meaning in all things. Acrabiel will bring to you the wisdom of the divine and help you apply this wisdom to your everyday living. When you apply divine wisdom to your life all falls into place and you achieve harmony and happiness. Acrabiel will be with you as you endeavour to achieve illumination which brings untold joy to the heart. Illumination is knowing that you are a child of the divine and looked after by angels and divine power that brings courage and inspiration to your heart. The indigo ray is a very powerful ray that awakens the mind in the heart. This spiritual mind is one with the divine mind and will bring meaning for life that the Scorpio soul has been searching for.

Indigo is a combination of the blue and violet rays, together creating a beautiful dark, deep blue. The indigo ray reflects the harmony and healing powers of the blue ray and the beauty and love of ceremony of the violet ray. Acrabiel will bring to the Scorpio healing powers that will fulfill your desire for service, which is quite important to the Scorpio soul. Acrabiel will also bring the opportunity for ritual and ceremony which is important to Scorpios who adapt well to religious concepts that include ritual and ceremony in their ways of worship. The Scorpio searches for meanings beyond the established religious institutions and looks for deeper and more secretive concepts of spiritual attainment. The new age is very much the thing for the Scorpio, and Acrabiel will lead you to find the path that fulfils your desire for spiritual illumination. Acrabiel understands the Scorpio's desire for the hidden knowledge of life and death and will lead you to find spiritual vision and revelation.

Meditation with Acrabiel and the colour indigo will bring renewed energy to you when you are feeling depleted in mind, body, or soul. Scorpios have large amounts of energy and like to be kept busy, but sometimes they are liable to overdo things and wear themselves out. At such times Acrabiel will come with his power and energy and revitalise ailing spirits, bringing new enthusiasm to live life to the fullest. Meditation with Acrabiel will renew your energy and will also uplift you if you are feeling down or depressed.

Scorpios are emotionally sensitive and can get hurt easily, but meditation with Acrabiel will bring healing to hurt emotions and his power will also sort out any problems that you have. It is sometimes difficult to let go of problems but Acrabiel will help the Scorpio release any negative energy that is causing distress and will heal the situation with his power and love. Acrabiel will lead the Scorpio to a peaceful and stress-free life with all things in harmony. Problems need not be all negative, for it is through mistakes that we grow and learn. Problems can lead us in new directions and with the help of Acrabiel this can be very positive. The Scorpio does at times tend to attract trouble, but with Acrabiel beside you, you will find that problems sort themselves out fairly rapidly. When in a difficult situation, just imagine a shining angel, Acrabiel, next to you wearing shimmering indigo robes. He comes to ease you through difficult situations. He is always with you and will guide you to a peaceful and purposeful life.

The first meditation with Acrabiel will bring you divine wisdom to realise your full potential in life. Acrabiel will help you in your quest for answers to spiritual questions and help you get to the heart of things and understand spiritual law. He will help you develop your intuition and healing gifts and will bring you a deep peace from which to live your life. Acrabiel will bring a completeness to your soul, for when you understand spiritual law, you can live your life truly as a child of the divine.

The second meditation with Acrabiel will restore energy to you when you are feeling depleted. It is not easy to live a happy and fulfilling life when we feel weakened in any way but Acrabiel will bring energy back to the soul and help you live to the maximum of your energies. Acrabiel is a wise and loving angel and will help you have integrity and determination in all that you do so that you balance your energies realistically and avoid overdoing it.

The third meditation with Acrabiel will help you sort out problems in your life. Acrabiel will bring a steadying influence to your life to help you avoid difficult situations and live a life of peace and tranquillity. He will also heal any hurts you are feeling and will restore balance and harmony to your life and affairs. Just imagine a symbol of the problem, be it financial or with a person, and hold it or them in the light of Acrabiel. You will be surprised how easily the problem resolves itself. If the problem is with a person, just imagine the person in the indigo light of Acrabiel, and he will help you see both sides of the problem. He will bring integrity and discrimination to your thinking and help you solve the problem in the most kind and thoughtful way.

Meditation to Develop Your Intuition

Make yourself comfortable and prepare yourself for meditation as suggested in the introduction. Before you stands Acrabiel in shimmering indigo robes. The indigo light enfolds you and you feel Acrabiel's power and love flowing through you. Your soul absorbs the wisdom of Acrabiel and you know that this wisdom will bring answers and direction to your life. Acrabiel's beautiful light brings a deep peace to your soul and you know that all will be well in your life. You know that through the power of Acrabiel you will find fulfilment and meaning, and answers will come to you. Acrabiel will bring illumination to your mind and soul and he will reveal to you the secrets of life that you have been searching for. Acrabiel brings the secrets of the mystics to your soul and enables you to reach a higher level of consciousness that reveals the secrets of the ages to your mind. Acrabiel enfolds you in his love and wisdom and you feel it permeating your deepest being. Acrabiel will develop your intuition to a higher level, and through this you will attain the wisdom of the ages. Hold this feeling for as long as you feel comfortable, then bring your awareness back to your actual surroundings.

Practice this meditation every day or until you feel you have completed your work with Acrabiel. He will bring you answers to your questions, so it is a good idea to have a note-book with you at all times for you never know when answers will come to you. You will find you have a new direction in life and that you will have the opportunity to express your spiritual powers. You will attain spiritual wisdom, and your life will be happy and fulfilled when you walk with Acrabiel by your side.

Meditation to Restore Energy and Bring Integrity and Determination

Sit comfortably and make yourself ready for meditation using the suggestions in the introduction. Imagine before you a beautiful angel dressed in shimmering indigo robes. This is Acrabiel, and he comes to give you his love and strength. He holds out his hands in love and greeting and you take them and feel his love and vitality flowing through you. When he enfolds you in his indigo light, you feel your spirits rise. His love and power revitalises your mind, body, and spirit, and you feel yourself rise above the cares of the everyday to a new feeling of love and courage. Acrabiel's power brings a new energy to your soul and tired mind and body, and you feel ready to cope with anything that life brings you. You have the integrity and determination to live wisely and to the best of your abilities. Hold this feeling for as long as you feel comfortable, then bring your awareness back to your actual surroundings.

Practice this meditation every day or until you feel better. Acrabiel's power will be with you whenever you feel down; just imagine him standing in front of you, radiating his powerful indigo ray of light.

Meditation to Solve Problems and Bring Tranquility When In a Stressful State

Make yourself comfortable and prepare yourself for meditation using the suggestions in the introduction. Imagine before you a beautiful angel dressed in indigo robes. This is Acrabiel, and he enfolds you in his love. Feel this love permeating every cell of your being, bringing a sense of deep peace and happiness to you. Imagine a symbol that represents the problem troubling you and hold it in your hands. Acrabiel shines his indigo light upon it and enfolds it with his wisdom and understanding. Know that all will be well and that Acrabiel will bring you the means to solve your problem in a positive way.

If the problem is with a person, imagine the person or persons standing between you and Acrabiel. He shines his indigo light on you and them and brings his love and wisdom to bear on the situation. Imagine silver threads connecting you to the person you are having the problem with, and imagine Acrabiel bringing his hand down three times to cut the threads that bind you together. Know that the problem will be solved in the most positive way with understanding and grace on both sides. Hold this feeling for as long as you feel comfortable, then bring your awareness back to your actual surroundings.

Practice this meditation every day until you feel the problem is solved. Acrabiel's power will bring a healing to your life, and his love will bring joy to your heart. His love for you is unconditional and will uplift you and bring you courage to live your life to the fullest of your capabilities. Problems will dissolve away, and you will live a life of harmony and peace with Acrabiel beside you.

Azrael, the Angel of Pluto

The Scorpion comes under the influence of the powerful ray of Pluto, and the angel of Pluto is Azrael, a kind and loving angel who will bring the wisdom of Pluto to the Scorpio soul. Pluto is on the wisdom ray, and Azrael will help the Scorpio soul to attain the highest forms of spiritual wisdom that will bring answers to the many questions the Scorpio asks about life and death.

Scorpio is the sign of secrets, and Pluto brings an urge to seek that which is hidden, unravel mysteries, and break new ground. Azrael will help the Scorpio soul seek wisely and to find answers to the many questions in the Scorpio mind.

Azrael is also known as the angel of death, but there is nothing sinister in this. Azrael is a kind and gentle angel who leads those who have passed over into the Summerland and the afterlife, soothing their fears and bringing the joy of release to their hearts. He is the comforter to those who pass into the light and brings his comfort to the Scorpion soul in times of need. He will bring the knowledge that the Scorpio soul is an eternal being and that there is nothing to fear in life or death.

Pluto, known as Hades to the ancient Greeks, rules the underworld in mythology. He also rules the underworld in the human soul—the subconscious. Deep within the subconscious lie the secrets of our past lives and our meaning for life in the present incarnation. Azrael will bring this knowledge to the Scorpio, who seeks for answers to the many questions about incarnation and so-called death.

Pluto brings a strong urge for self-expression as well as courage, energy, independence, and drive to the Scorpio personality; Azrael will bring these aspects to the Scorpio soul and help develop their talents and let their spirits soar to new heights.

With Azrael beside you, your Scorpio soul can realise all its dreams and live a life of harmony and deep happiness, for Azrael brings true knowledge to the Scorpio, knowledge that he/she has been seeking. Finding this knowledge brings joy to the heart. Azrael will bring new heights of self-expression to the Scorpio soul and will bring the power for his/her talents to flourish.

With the knowledge of the secrets of life and death comes wisdom, and Azrael will help the Scorpion soul use this knowledge wisely for the benefit of all that Scorpios come into contact with. Azrael brings the secret of turning base metal into gold, the transformation of the earthly personality into a compassionate, loving, and wise spiritual being. This is what the Scorpio has incarnated to learn, and this is his/her lesson in this life. When the Scorpio has achieved this, untold joy will come to the heart for he/ she will be a vehicle for the love and wisdom of the divine. Azrael will be beside you as you endeavour to live up to these ideals and will bring you inner strength and courage to live life according to the laws of spiritual illumination.

The meditation with Azrael will bring you the wisdom and knowledge of the divine as well as answers where there is confusion and unknowing. Azrael will bring a sense of well-being to your soul and will enfold you in his love, bringing strength and courage to your heart to follow your goals and aspirations in life. His power will bring spiritual fulfilment, and you will learn the secrets of your spirit and the secrets of this incarnation on earth.

Azrael is commonly depicted in black robes, but I find this colour too powerful for meditation. I always see Azrael attired in deep rose-coloured robes, the colour of wisdom, love, and also healing. Whatever colour you see him dressed in, he will bring his love and wisdom to your soul and will help you find expression for your spiritual ideals, thereby creating a fulfilling and happy life.

Meditation for Learning the Secrets of Your Spirit and the Reason for Your Present Incarnation

Sit comfortably and prepare yourself for meditation as suggested in the introduction. When you feel ready, imagine standing before you a magnificent angel dressed in deep rose-coloured robes radiating a soft rose light. This is Azrael, who holds out his hands in love and greeting. Take his hands and feel his power and love flowing through every part of you. Feel yourself enveloped in a rose-coloured light and know that Azrael brings his wisdom and spiritual knowledge to your mind. He will bring answers to your questions and inner strength and courage to live up to your ideals. Know that Azrael will bring you the secrets of your spirit and knowledge of your reasons for incarnating on earth. He will help you live a life of harmony and happiness, for when one has spiritual illumination, all becomes clear and the love at your heart centre can blossom and flourish. This brings untold happiness to you, and you know that all is well in your life.

Hold the feeling of being enfolded in Azrael's rose-coloured light for as long as is comfortable, then bring your awareness back to your actual surroundings. Practice this meditation as often as you wish until you feel your work with Azrael is done. He will be beside you as go about your daily life, inspiring you and helping you achieve spiritual wholeness. His wisdom will come to you to answer your questions and you will grow in spiritual awareness that brings a joy to your heart. This joy can really be felt for it is very real and you will find your life becomes more meaningful and fulfilled.

9
Sagittarius

Medonial, the Angel of Caring

The special angel of Sagittarius is Medonial, the angel of caring. He is a very loving angel who will bring the wisdom of caring to the Sagittarian soul. Medonial will bring the realisation that caring about people brings us into focus in life. When we care, what happens to those we care about affects us, and Medonial will help us direct our prayers and intentions towards achieving healing and happiness for those around us. Caring means that we are concerned for the wellbeing and happiness of others, and Medonial will guide us to care wisely and bring our love to bear in a positive manner.

It comes easily to the Sagittarius character to care for others, for theirs is an outgoing and positive personality who cares passionately about others. Medonial will help you direct your passionate nature to do the most good and will help you direct your enthusiasm for life to good causes.

The ability to care reflects a warm and passionate heart and Medonial will enrich these feelings and bring to your soul the ability to care about what happens in life. He will bring the lesson that your values in life are positive and good and not based on falsehoods and misrepresentations.

By caring you align yourself with the angels, for they care deeply about mankind. Medonial cares deeply about you and will bring his love and caring to work positive magic in your life. When we care we attract people into our lives who care about us. Being cared for brings a warmth to the heart because it brings a feeling of positive love to our emotions, affirming that we are working from the highest ideals. Caring is the opposite of the selfish, materialistic values of modern society. Medonial will steer you away from such values and lead you to a path of compassion and caring that will bring a joy to your heart, as caring enriches our lives.

Caring passionately about people opens up the heart centre and lets in the light of the divine that brings its divine wisdom. When our heart centre is ruled by the divine light, wisdom follows, for we are affirming that we are actively turning away from negative responses. Medonial will help you to let go of any negative emotions and reactions that you have and to open your heart centre to the light. Caring affirms that you are working from the highest ideals and that you are a compassionate and whole human being.

It is good to feel cared for, and no one in the world should feel that they lack care. There are many in the world today who need our care and compassion, and we can show our caring by supporting just causes. Sending light and love out into the world by way of prayer is an affirmation of caring, and Medonial will help you to do this by a simple meditation of sending out the light. Meditation with Medonial will deepen your caring attitude and he will also bring his wisdom to your soul, for when we care we can feel deep sadness at the injustice in the world. Such negative feelings do no good for they do not creative a positive outlook. Medonial will help you always feel positive and will lessen your feelings of sadness and even outrage at the extent of injustice in the world. Medonial will bring his caring to you, and you will feel a warmth at your heart centre and a knowing that all humanity is loved and cared for by angels. Even in the darkest of times the angels are with mankind to bring courage and fortitude, and the caring of angels brings a positive outcome for many.

Caring for ourselves is very important, and Medonial will bring his love to you to help you care for yourself. Sometimes people spend so much time caring for others that they neglect themselves, which is not in the divine way of things. Caring for ourselves is very important, for it affirms we are a child of God and that our caring is an extension of divine love and wisdom. We need to feel good about ourselves and Medonial will help you view yourself in a new light. Many people neglect themselves, for they do not feel good enough in their own eyes, but this is a negative attitude and denies that we are children of God. Medonial will help you have respect for yourself and take care of yourself in a positive manner, for by not caring for yourself you are denying the care of the angels. Really taking care of yourself will bring you a more positive outlook and help you in caring for others.

Medonial will bring the divine light to your soul, for caring is one of the greatest gifts we can give to the world. It reflects in how we live our lives. By caring the angels can draw near and help to bring about happiness and fulfilment, and Medonial will always be by your side to bring inspiration and give support.

Meditation to Send Love and Light Into the World and Learn the True Meaning of Caring

Sit comfortably and make yourself ready for meditation by using the suggestions in the introduction. Imagine standing in front of you a beautiful, tall angel dressed in rose-coloured robes, the colour of love and caring. Imagine a beautiful rose that is a deep shade of pink—this is the colour of this angel. This is Medonial, and he comes to help you use your caring talents for the good of all mankind. He enfolds you in his soft rose light that permeates every cell of your being. Feel this light flowing through you, bringing a deep sense of peace and love for yourself, for all you know, and for all creation. Feel this light at your heart centre opening up your heart to the love of the divine and see this light radiating out from you and flowing into the world. You care about humanity and all creation and this is expressed in your love that now flows to the world. Don't worry about the light going to any particular place, for Medonial will know where best to use it. This is your gift to the world, and it brings a complete joy to your heart to be doing this work accompanied by Medonial. You will understand the true meaning of caring and it will bring you to a higher state of consciousness and understanding of spiritual laws.

Hold this feeling of sending the rose light out into the world for as long as you feel comfortable and then bring your awareness back to your actual surroundings. Practice this meditation as often as you feel you would like to, for it is doing good work in the world. Angel work is very powerful, and someone somewhere will be touched by your rose light. The work will bring joy to your heart, and you will find that such work has its effect on your personal life. You will become more loving and caring and will experience a deep peace and inspiration for living your life. It will strengthen your bond with Medonial who will be beside you every day to bring his wisdom and his love to you and help you in your everyday living. You will find that problems in your life melt away and that you are able to live a positive and constructive life with the angels beside you.

Chesetiel, the Angel of the Gold Ray

Sagittarians are working under the gold ray, and the angel of the gold ray is Chesetiel, a very loving and powerful angel who will bring to the Sagittarian soul the warmth and positive outlook of this brilliant colour. It is the colour of the sun and is associated with masculine energy no matter your gender.

Chesetiel will help you work with the gold ray in your life, for it is a ray that will inspire you to higher ideals and encourage you to a deeper knowledge of your inner spirit and soul. The gold ray brings wisdom to the soul, and Chesetiel will inspire you to use this wisdom wisely in your daily life. The gold ray brings the desire for spiritual knowledge and understanding of spiritual laws, and Chesetiel will bring these to you and help you live your life to the ultimate of spiritual truth.

The gold ray is one of passion and generosity, and as we have seen with the angel of caring, Sagittarians are working towards compassion and the high ideals of caring and understanding of spiritual law. Gold inspires warmth of personality, a generous outlook, and a loving nature. Chesetiel will help you develop these ideals and bring a deep peace and joy to your heart as you fulfill your soul's desires.

The gold ray is the ray of wealth and material richness, so if you are suffering a lack of money in your life meditating on the gold ray will help reverse your fortunes and bring wealth into your life. Chesetiel will inspire you to an optimistic outlook and help you attract money into your life. He will assist you to look at your life and see where changes can be made to attract more richness, and he will help promote a positive outlook, for a negative outlook will not attract good things to you. Chesetiel will bring the abundance of gold into your life and the power of gold will bring good fortune and happiness where there might be despair. Chesetiel will uplift you and bring his magic to your soul. Meditation with him will bring a deep joy to your heart, for it will bring the brilliance of gold to your soul. If you are suffering a lack of money, the gold ray is an ideal colour to work with, as it represents wealth, prosperity, affluence, and luxury. The meditation with Chesetiel will help you achieve success and attract gold into your life in the form of abundance and wealth.

Many people on the spiritual path have a problem with wealth, regarding it as unspiritual or unimportant to be rich, but this is not the case: you can be rich and very spiritual because it is not the acquisition of money that has a negative aspect. It is the greed for money and the means by which you achieve your abundance that is the problem. Chesetiel will be beside you to help you achieve abundance and will guide you to act in accordance with your highest ideals and lead a happy and rewarding life.

The gold ray also brings energy back to depleted souls. If you are feeling exhausted by doing too much or after suffering an illness, meditation with Chesetiel on the gold ray will bring renewed energy to your tired mind and body. Gold is the colour of the sun, and all the energy of the sun will come to you as you meditate with Chesetiel. Such meditation will soon lift your spirits and bring a refreshed outlook to life, and you will soon find you can go about your daily tasks with newfound vigour and optimism that will bring a sparkle to your soul.

The gold ray will also sort out any problems you may have. Chesetiel will bring his wisdom and his power to any problems you are experiencing and causing you distress. It is through our problems and trials that we grow and learn and through the love of Chesetiel the lesson of the problem will reveal itself to you in the most harmonious way. The colour gold will shine on your problem and resolve it, for you bring the wisdom of the divine to your mind and heart. Just imagine a symbol that represents your problem and hold it in the light of Chesetiel and you will be surprised how quickly the problem develops into a satisfactory conclusion. If it is a person you are having problems with Chesetiel will bring his love and wisdom to the situation and brings about a harmonising of the problem. Through the divine love of Chesetiel, you will live a harmonious, peaceful, and happy life. When problems arise, just imagine them in the light of Chesetiel and harmony will be restored for the good of all concerned.

The first meditation with Chesetiel will bring richness and prosperity into your life because when you meditate on the gold ray, you attract all the power of gold to you. Chesetiel will help you have a positive outlook regarding money, and if you are suffering a lack, he will reverse your fortunes with his wisdom and love. Lack of money brings distress, which is not in the plan of the divine for your life. Chesetiel will address the problem and bring the richness of gold to your soul and help you resolve all the problems you have with money. When we have richness in our life, we are in tune with the divine plan, for it is not in the divine plan that we be distressed or lacking in anything.

The second meditation with Chesetiel will bring energy to you when you are feeling exhausted and depleted in vitality. He will bring the power of gold, the colour of the sun, to your body, mind, and soul; you will find you have newfound vigour after meditation with Chesetiel and the golden ray. Chesetiel will bring a deep strength to our soul to live your life to the fullest of your abilities and the golden ray will bring inspiration to your soul to work from the very heart of your being.

The third meditation with Chesetiel and the gold ray will help solve any problems you are experiencing. Chesetiel will restore harmony to your life and bring about a resolution of any disharmony bringing distress to your soul.

The fourth meditation with Chesetiel will bring wisdom to your soul and help you live your life in a positive and inspirational manner. He will inspire you with spiritual truths and help you live your life in harmony with those spiritual truths so that joy and love envelop your heart and mind.

Meditation to Bring Abundance and Prosperity Into Your Life

Make yourself comfortable and prepare yourself for meditation as detailed in the introduction. Imagine standing before you an angel dressed in bright golden robes radiating a shining golden light. This is Chesetiel, and he greets you by enfolding you in his love. His golden light enfolds you and permeates every cell of your being. Feel it radiating throughout your physical body and your mental body and soul. This golden light melts away any negative feelings about money and attracts to you wealth and prosperity. Know that from now on the golden power of Chesetiel will work for you to create abundance and richness in your life. Imagine the light from Chesetiel as a wonderful gold, the colour of wealth and luxury. Know these things will be yours with the help of Chesetiel, who will be beside you every day to help attract to you all the wealth and richness you require. Imagine yourself breathing in the golden light and see it radiating throughout your body. You radiate this golden light in your aura and as you do so, you attract gold. Hold these feelings for as long as you feel comfortable then bring your awareness back to your actual surroundings.

Practice this meditation every day for maximum effect and you will soon find that your wealth increases and that money problems dissolve away. Thank Chesetiel for his help and give him your love. He will be beside you to bring the power of gold into your life and bring wealth, luxury, and abundance to you.

Meditation to Bring the Energy of the Sun to a Depleted Soul

Sit comfortably and prepare yourself for meditation by using the techniques detailed in the introduction. Imagine standing before you a beautiful angel dressed in glowing golden robes. This is Chesetiel, and he comes to bring you love and energy. He radiates a golden light that enfolds you and permeates every cell of your being. Feel this golden light as an energy flowing through your veins, bringing a renewed sense of vitality. Feel the light flowing through your mental body and your soul, revitalising your tired body and mind. Feel the light as golden sunshine with the power of the golden sun radiating through you bringing new vigour to your whole being. Hold these feelings for as long as they are comfortable then bring your awareness back to your actual surroundings.

Practice this meditation every day until you feel better and thank Chesetiel for his help. When you feel down or at a low ebb, just imagine the golden sunshine of Chesetiel enfolding you and flowing through you restoring a well-balanced equilibrium to your whole being.

Meditation to Solve Problems

Make yourself comfortable and prepare yourself for meditation using the suggestions in the introduction. In front of you stands Chesetiel radiating a beautiful golden light that enfolds you and fills you with love. Feel this golden light flowing through you, empowering you and bringing a positive feeling to your emotions. Imagine a symbol for the problem you are having and see this symbol in front of you. The golden light of Chesetiel enfolds this symbol and irradiates it with power and love. Know that the problem will resolve itself in the best possible way and that any distress you feel over the problem will be eased away in the powerful golden light of Chesetiel. Know that all is well and that Chesetiel brings harmony to your life. Hold these feelings for as long as they feel comfortable and then bring your awareness back to your actual surroundings.

Repeat this meditation until you feel the problem has resolved itself. You will find the problem sorts itself out in the best possible way and that you have peace and harmony in your life. Problems come to give us lessons on the spiritual path, and Chesetiel will bring his wisdom to you so you can understand the lesson that was inherent in this problem. He will help you gain wisdom and a knowledge of spiritual law that governs all our lives.

Meditation to Gain Divine Wisdom

Make yourself comfortable and if you wish, prepare yourself for meditation as suggested in the introduction. See standing before you a magnificent golden angel radiating a golden light that enfolds you in his love and power. This is Chesetiel, and he gives you all his love. Feel his power flowing through you and into your aura and know that his deep wisdom is yours to experience and understand. Chesetiel brings knowledge to your mind, a knowledge of the higher spiritual laws by which you want to live your life. He will help you and inspire you as you reach upwards to these higher ideals, and he will bring to your heart the divine love of God. Chesetiel will reveal to you the secrets of spiritual law and bring the wisdom of the ages to your mind. He will lift you to a higher level of consciousness and spiritual awareness that will bring harmony and happiness to your life. You feel uplifted and joyous at these revelations. Hold these feelings for as long as you feel comfortable and then bring your awareness back to your actual surroundings.

Keep a notebook handy over the next few days, for ideas and spiritual truths will come to you as Chesetiel inspires you with spiritual wisdom. Practice the meditation every day if you wish and you will find a deep peace settles within you as you understand that you are a magnificent being, a child of God who has the power to bring harmony and joyousness to your life.

Sachiel, the Angel of Jupiter

Sagittarians come under the influence of Jupiter and the angel of Jupiter is Sachiel, a wise and loving angel who will bring to the Sagittarian soul all the wisdom of Jupiter. The planet Jupiter increases the hopeful, sociable, joyous side of the Sagittarian nature and brings material prosperity. The influence of Jupiter works more through feeling, impulse, and intuition rather than through reason, which means Sagittarians will often have hunches or moments of insight, which in a material way can bring good luck. But at the back of the Sagittarian mind will be the thought that perhaps there is a force or power that brings good luck. This brings a desire to know the truth of such a power, and Sachiel will guide you to seek out the secrets of the divine that has so much influence on your life.

Sachiel brings aspiration to the Sagittarian soul and he brings the desire to understand divine law and a desire to probe the depths of the soul and the reason for your life. Sachiel will bring his wisdom to the Sagittarian soul and bring about a realisation of the true meaning of life and death. Jupiter is essentially the planet of religion in all its forms, and the Sagittarian seeks profound knowledge of the mysteries of spiritual truth. Sachiel will help all those who seek divine truth and will bring determination and commitment to follow a spiritual path and live up to ideals of the higher nature. The influence of Jupiter means that the Sagittarian can obtain illumination of the spiritual life by sudden conversion after having experienced the touch of angel's wings by intuitive awareness or feels by intuition the joy of divine love. This altruistic love can bring the light of enlightenment to the soul and a determination to seek the supreme source of the light that has been glimpsed.

Sachiel will bring to the Sagittarian soul all the wisdom of divine power as the need to progress spiritually deepens in your heart. This desire will motivate you to release yourself from the confines of orthodoxy, for those under the ray of Jupiter cannot be bound within narrow limits and know that there are greater degrees of spiritual illumination to be discovered. The Sagittarian must be free to discover spiritual truths in his/her own way. Sachiel will be with you to guide you as you set out on a spiritual journey to discover the source of the light that you have glimpsed. When one has seen this light the only desire is to reach the source and become one with that light and to convey to others the magnificent truth of spiritual enlightenment. Sachiel will guide you to use your natural abilities of intuition and intellectual knowledge to express this knowledge and help others reach the same heights of spiritual awareness that you have achieved.

With such illumination comes great joy, for you realise you are one with all creation and that you are held in the divine love of the supreme being. Sachiel will guide you along your chosen pathway and bring to you the deepest revelations of spiritual knowledge that you are searching for. The meditation with Sachiel will bring illumination to your mind and soul and answer the questions you have been asking yourself. When you have found this illumination harmony will reign in your life, for you will be radiating a golden aura of positivity, peace, and love and no harm can come to you with the angels walking by your side. Sachiel will bring the realisation that all creation has the divine light deep within them and that all creation is as one in the light of the divine.

Sachiel will help the Sagittarian develop intuition and will guide you to mastery over the lower self whereby you come under the total power of the higher self. In alchemy, this is the turning of the base metal into pure gold, the colour of Sagittarius, and Sachiel will be by your side to help you attain this highest of ideals.

Meditation to Bring Unity with Divine Light

Sit comfortably and prepare yourself for meditation by using the techniques suggested in the introduction. Before you stands a beautiful angel dressed in shining golden robes. This is Sachiel, the angel of Jupiter, and he enfolds you in his golden ray of love. Feel this love permeating your entire body and mind and feel the power of Sachiel flowing through you. His wisdom enfolds you and brings to your being the knowledge of divine truth. Sachiel reveals the divine light that shines within you and brings to your soul divine wisdom and divine love. Through Sachiel's power, this divine light within you is stimulated and grows until it illuminates your entire being and brings spiritual knowledge and truth to your mind. You feel a great joy as this light within floods your whole being and you know that you are a magnificent child of the divine, an eternal being, shining with the light of the divine. Hold this feeling for as long as you are comfortable, then bring your awareness back to your actual surroundings.

Practice this meditation as often as you wish and keep a notebook handy, for divine truths will come to you as you go about your daily life. You will attain the spiritual truths that you have been searching for and will receive spiritual illumination that reveals you are one with the divine. The joy you felt in the meditation and the spiritual awareness that you experienced will remain with you and you will live a more harmonious life as you are radiating the light of the divine. Happiness and prosperity will be yours, for you are radiating positive vibrations that attract positive happenings back into your life.

Adnachiel, the Angel of Sacrifice

The special lesson that Sagittarians have incarnated to learn is one of sacrifice, and the angel of sacrifice is Adnachiel, a powerful and loving angel who will help Sagittarians in their quest for the highest of ideals.

Sacrifice does not mean giving up all worldly pleasures and living a life of denial and lack. We incarnate to enjoy life, make the very best of our talents, and use those talents for the good of society. Adnachiel will guide you to live a happy and prosperous life making the best of your gifts for the benefit of yourself and your family.

The sacrifice you have incarnated to learn is that of the lower nature, and Adnachiel will help you understand what this entails. The lower nature is our desire nature, the part of us that craves power and material gain. Adnachiel will guide you to realise that the sacrifice of this nature brings us into a state of happiness that cannot be gained by material success alone. By letting go of the desire nature, we are making a commitment to being spiritual beings and that avowing that we are one with the divine. The desire for material things cannot bring true happiness, only more desire, but once you have let go of the desire nature, sacrificed it for the higher nature that is one with the divine, true happiness can enter your soul and the real meaning of sacrifice comes to you.

Sacrifice of the lower personality is a development from the progress you have made spiritually with the angel of Jupiter. As you work more and more from the higher self and from the ideals of spiritual laws learned through enlightenment, you will naturally be shedding the restrictions and distractions of the lower personality. Adnachiel will guide you to live up to your ideals of the higher spiritual nature and will assist you in sacrificing your lower nature for the good of your being. This will be easy, for once you have glimpsed the light of the divine and experienced the great joy this brings, the joy of material possessions will diminish. This does not mean you will have to live frugally. Quite the opposite, for when one is living from the light of your divine nature, prosperity and wealth will naturally become yours as you are attracting good things into your life by radiating positive vibrations.

Adnachiel will bring to your soul the wisdom of the divine and will help you as you let go of your lower nature. He will bring your soul great joy, for letting go of the lower nature means you are letting go of all its fears and anxieties. Adnachiel will bring you the truth that the higher nature does not know fear, anxiety, resentments, or anger, for it is part of the divine and the divine is complete and forever positive. You will find your relationships become happier and more harmonious and Adnachiel will guide you to always keep a positive outlook.

Adnachiel will bring you the realisation that true sacrifice on the spiritual path is a positive and wonderful development of spiritual law because when you are living from the highest in you, that higher self rules the lower self and makes it impossible to be negative in any way. True happiness comes when the lower self is sacrificed to the higher self and Adnachiel will bring this wonderful truth to your being. By sacrificing our low self we are affirming that divine love rules our heart and mind. This brings true happiness for by radiating divine love you will attract more love into your life.

True sacrifice of the lower nature occurs when one has found spiritual enlightenment. After the meditation with Sachiel, you will be prepared to let go of all your negative thoughts and ideas. Sacrifice of the lower nature will become easy, for Adnachiel will help as you let go of negative emotions. The unfoldment of your spiritual nature will be complete and Adnachiel will reveal to you the light of the spirit that holds all secrets of your real nature and your reasons for your being. True joy will come to your heart, for you no longer desire that which is impossible and no longer have negative emotions to distress and impair your daily life. By sacrificing your lower nature, you are affirming your oneness with the divine and that you are going to be true to the light that you developed with Sachiel, the angel of Jupiter. Adnachiel will guide you to a happier and more positive lifestyle where your true wonderful nature will flourish. The supreme happiness that comes from being at one with the divine will envelope you and you will become a beacon of light for all who know you.

Meditation to Learn the True Nature of Sacrifice and Obtain Union with Your Higher Self

Make yourself comfortable and prepare for meditation by using the techniques set out in the introduction. Before you stands a beautiful angel dressed in golden robes that radiate a deep golden glow. This is Adnachiel, and he has come to help you let go of your desire body and live from your higher self and divine love. Feel his power and love enfolding you and flowing throughout your entire being. His light lifts you up into a great joy, and you know that you are one with the divine power and have everything you need. You will attract good things into your life because you will be working from the highest in you. Adnachiel will bring his wisdom to your mind and his love to your heart and you will live life to your fullest potential and abilities. Hold these feelings for as long as it is comfortable, then bring your awareness back to your actual surroundings.

Practice this meditation every day to feel the love of Adnachiel working its magic in your life. He will bring joy to your heart and you will find that your life flows easily and harmoniously. All will be well, and you will experience a great relief as you let go of the the lower self's anxieties and fears, instead putting your trust in the angels. Adnachiel will be beside you to lift up your spirits and bring you happiness and joy as you live from the highest ideals and the positive power of the higher self.

10
Capricorn

Shenial, the Angel of Pleasure

The special angel of Capricorn is Shenial, the angel of pleasure, a wise and loving angel who will bring the experience of real pleasure to the Capricornian soul. Pleasure is a God-given gift that can sustain us during negative times in our lives. When things go wrong, doing something pleasurable can uplift us to view life with a new perspective and give us inspiration to put things right. Shenial will reveal to you the simplicity of pleasure in our lives when all our senses are in accord and our spirit soars above the mundane of everyday living.

Pleasure puts us in touch with our spirit—it opens up that which is positive in our lives. Shenial will help you experience the true meaning of pleasure and bring about positive happenings in your life. The angels rejoice when we are happy and experiencing pleasure, for it means we are rising above the lower self (full of fears and anxieties) and experiencing the joy of the higher senses.

Shenial is a beautiful angel and he will encourage you to seek that which is pleasurable in your life. Pleasure is often felt through the simple things of life and can act as a balm when things are going wrong in our lives. Pleasure is a respite from the everyday, but we can make mundane things in our daily lives into pleasurable acts. Shenial will show you how to experience pleasure by doing the simplest things, such as helping others or your daily chores. Shenial will help you experience these activities in a different light. When we bring pleasure into our lives, we are experiencing the will of God, for it is his will that we should be happy and feeling pleasure rather than the negative emotions of depression and despondency.

Shenial will teach you that pleasure will bring you into awareness of your spirit and help you rise above the lower self. When you open yourself to pleasure, you affirm that you are a child of God. Shenial will help you realise what you really want out of life. We are living our life from the highest ideals when we experience pleasure, for pleasure is a guide to how we should be living. Shenial will bring to your soul the knowledge that pleasure is of God and that his will is that we should be happy through pleasurable things.

Pleasure teaches us that we are children of God and that the simplest things in life can bring us happiness and pleasure.

How much pleasure do you have in your life? Shenial will bring to your awareness the fact that pleasure is full of the possibilities of expansion of the soul. This will lift you into the realms of the divine where true pleasure will bring you the happiness that is your right as a child of God. What gives you pleasure in life? Do these things with gratitude to God for his gifts that bring so much pleasure to your life. You are living from the highest in you when you do things that give you pleasure but it needs to be used wisely. Shenial will bring you the ability to trust in the truths of your heart and to bring pleasure to your life whatever the circumstances.

Take time out from your daily tasks to commune with Shenial in the beautiful garden of the angels. Experience the pleasure of just being and absorb the wisdom and love of your angel which will bring so much wisdom and love to your soul.

Meditation to Experience More Pleasure in Your Life and Understand the True Meaning of Pleasure

Sit comfortably and prepare for meditation following the suggestions in the introduction. Before you stands a beautiful angel radiating a soft rose-coloured light. This is Shenial, and he enfolds you in his light. Feel this soft rose light permeating every cell of your being. Relax in this light and enjoy just being yourself. Be aware of your deepest feelings and reflect for a while on who you really are—a child of God, perfect in every way.

Absorb into your soul the wisdom and love of Shenial and be aware of the pleasure it gives you to sit in this beautiful garden and commune with your special angel. Feel his love and return your love to him. Feel a deep love for yourself and feel at peace with yourself and know that all is well in your life. Hold this feeling for as long as is comfortable then bring your awareness back to your actual surroundings.

The effect of this meditation will be that you will be able to think more clearly and sort out any problems you are having in your life. You will feel more at ease with yourself and more self-confident for you will be relating to your higher self. Shenial will be beside you to give his wisdom and love to uplift you and help you experience the expansion of pleasure within your soul.

Gediel, the Angel of the Purple Ray

The colour ray that Capricorn is working under is the purple ray and the angel of the purple ray is Gediel. The colour purple is the colour of the imagination and spirituality, and Gediel will assist you as you seek the meaning of life and spiritual unfoldment. The purple ray will expand your awareness of spiritual laws and ideals and will help connect you to your higher consciousness.

Gediel will help you expand your imagination, for without imagination you could not commune with the angels. Our imagination is a precious gift that brings into being our deepest held dreams. What we think we become so it is essential that our imaginings are positive and good. Gediel will bring his power to bear upon our imaginings to ensure they are of the highest ideals. Without imagination you could not imagine the angels who come to help you, for your imagination brings the angels into reality.

The purple ray brings the desire for meanings of life and Gediel will bring this knowledge to you and help you as you search for the truth of your being. This truth is that you are a child of God, perfect in every way. You may not think that you are perfect but Gediel will reveal to you the fact that imperfections are illusions and that at your deepest level you are a wonderful and perfect child of the divine. You are a person of two selves, the lower self which you know as your everyday personality and the higher self that is purely spiritual and knows the secrets of the spiritual laws and ideals and is the perfect child of God. Your higher consciousness also knows the secrets of why you have incarnated specifically as you have and understands the secrets of the Universe. Union with this higher consciousness is the aim of all on the spiritual path, and Gediel will bring his power to you and help you contact that higher part of you that is one with God. When one experiences union with the higher consciousness a wonderful joy comes to the soul, for you know that nothing can really harm you and you know the meaning of your life and what is needed to bring fulfillment to your being. Gediel will bring this knowledge to your soul and help you as you strive for spiritual knowledge. When you are living from the higher consciousness everything falls into place in your life and you know the full meaning of your life. You know why you have incarnated and what the lessons are that you have incarnated to learn. These lessons become enjoyable and meaningful and Gediel will guide you to live your life to your highest standards and have the courage to put those standards into practical being in your everyday life. The purple ray inspires unconditional love for all creation, which is the highest ideal you can aspire to. Unconditional love encourages compassion and sensitivity, which will bring to your understanding the true meaning of caring and loving. Unconditional love is the love of God and is the love your angels give you. You are held in unconditional love, for the angels know your innermost being. This love brings the greatest joy. When you love unconditionally you are affirming you are a true child of the divine.

The meditation with Gediel will help you make contact with your higher consciousness and bring this consciousness into your everyday living. He will teach you the reasons for your life and show you that the ego with its fears and frets and anxieties can be overcome by the higher consciousness, which will bring joy and harmony to your soul. Purple is the colour of harmony of the mental and physical being and this will bring peace of mind and the knowledge that putting your trust in angels, and Gediel, will bring a wonderful release from the negative emotions of the lower self. The meditation with Gediel will bring a deep harmony to your soul and bring about a union of the physical being with the higher spiritual self that is part of God. Once this union is reality you live from the highest ideals and your true nature can blossom and flourish and bring a great joy to your heart.

The colour purple will also bring energy to the mind and body when you are feeling depleted, and Gediel will restore your energy balance. It is all too easy to become negative when feeling worn out and exhausted, but Gediel will bring his power to your soul and refresh your spirit and emotions. The colour purple has a richness to it that inspires growth and enthusiasm. It is made up of the vibrant, energetic red ray and the calm and thoughtful blue ray and these qualities harmonise in the purple ray to bring a vitality that has integrity. Gediel will bring this harmony to your soul and uplift your emotions when you are feeling down. He will restore your equilibrium and bring about a new awareness and enthusiasm for life.

Gediel will also help you to sort out any problems you are having in your life. The purple ray is the ray of harmony, and Gediel will restore harmony to your life and bring about a resolution to those things that may be causing you distress. He will unite you to your higher spiritual consciousness which is capable of bringing inspiration to your lower mind, enabling you to bring about balance and happiness once more to your life. Mistakes help us grow as individuals and negative happenings are lessons that help us progress along the spiritual path. Gediel will inspire you to learn and move on from distressing incidents and happenings, and he will encourage you to look forward instead of back at mistakes and to look to the future with enthusiasm and courage.

The first meditation with Gediel will bring union with the higher consciousness and reveal to you the secrets of your life. Gediel will bring his wisdom to your soul and bring you spiritual knowledge that will reveal the secrets of the divine. The meditation will also assist you to use your imagination wisely, for imagination creates our lives.

The second meditation with Gediel will restore energy to your body and mind when you are feeling depleted. When you are tired you cannot function fully as a complete and confident human being but Gediel will bring balance back to your energy levels and restore a feeling of enthusiasm for living life to the fullest.

The third meditation with Gediel will bring wisdom to your soul to sort out any problems you are experiencing. His love will ease distress and bring harmony to the situation and a deep peace back to your soul.

Meditation to Bring Union with the Higher Consciousness

Make yourself comfortable and prepare for meditation using the suggestions detailed in the introduction. Imagine standing before you a beautiful angel dressed in sparkling purple robes. This is Gediel, and he enfolds you in purple light that permeates every cell of your being. Feel his love and his power flowing through you bringing inspiration and love to your soul. Feel this light radiating from your body to encompass your whole aura and know that the wisdom of Gediel is bringing spiritual knowledge that will bring you to the realisation of the true meaning of your life. Feel the purple ray of Gediel reaching deep into you and releasing the knowledge of the secrets of your incarnation and inspiring enthusiasm and courage to live your life to the fullest you can. Hold yourself in the light of Gediel and feel this purple ray stimulating your higher consciousness into union with your physical being and bringing spiritual fulfillment to your mind and soul. Know that answers and knowledge will come to you from Gediel and that all is well in your life. Hold these feelings for as long as you feel comfortable then bring your awareness back to your actual surroundings.

This meditation will expand your awareness of spiritual truths and bring about the knowledge you have been seeking. It is a powerful meditation that brings results. You will find that your life will be more harmonious and exciting for you will be living your life from the positive powerhouse of your higher consciousness. You will also find that you are able to imagine clearly positive happenings in your life. The power of your imagination will create a happy and harmonious life for you; all negativity will dissolve away and you will find you are leading a positive and worthwhile life that brings great joy to your heart. It is a good idea to keep a notebook and pen with you at all times for answers and truths will start to come to you as you go about your daily life. Practice the meditation daily and you will find a deep peace and newfound enthusism, and you will blossom into your true self as a child of God.

Meditation to Balance Energy Levels and Bring Energy to a Depleted Soul

Sit comfortably and make yourself ready for meditation by using the techniques detailed in the introduction. Before you stands a beautiful angel dressed in purple robes. This is Gediel, and he comes to give his love and power to you and bring energy to your depleted mind, body, and soul. He is surrounded by a soft purple light and radiates this light and enfolds you in it. Feel the power of Gediel permeating every cell of your being, bringing a new found energy and enthusiasm for life. Feel the love and power of Gediel suffusing your entire being and radiating throughout your aura. Feel his power bringing new vitality to your body and mind. You feel energised and ready to tackle all your tasks in your life. The power of Gediel brings a positive attitude to your mind and you feel a great joy that all is well in your life. Hold these feelings for as long as you feel comfortable then bring your awareness back to your actual surroundings.

Practice this meditation daily until you feel your energy has returned and you are facing your challenges with a new enthusiasm. Whenever you feel down imagine Gediel beside you giving you his power to lift you up and bring a passion for living your life to the fullest.

Meditation to Sort Our Problems in Your Life

Make yourself comfortable and prepare for meditation as suggested in the introduction. Before you stands Gediel clothed in beautiful purple robes, and he radiates a soft purple light that enfolds you and permeates every cell of your being. You feel at peace and know that Gediel will restore harmony to your life and to your soul. Imagine a symbol of the problem that bothers you and see it on the floor in front of you. Gediel shines his light upon it and you know that all will be well in your life. If it is a person you are having a problem with imagine that person standing before Gediel. Gediel enfolds the person in his love and power and you know that all will be resolved. Gediel brings you inspiration and clarity of mind to deal with the problem in the most harmonious way for all involved. You know that the problem is solved and that Gediel will bring his power and love to your soul to help you forgive and give your love to all concerned.

Hold these feelings for as long as you feel comfortable and then bring your awareness back to your actual surroundings. Practice this meditation every day until the problem is solved. You will find that harmony will soon be restored to your life in the most amazing way and that your life will be happier and more at peace.

Uriel, the Angel of Wisdom

The special lesson that Capricornians have incarnated to learn is that of wisdom. The angel of wisdom is Uriel whose name means "God is my light," for he shines the light of truth into the darkness of confusion and chaos. He will come to you when you have problems and need the wisdom of God to sort things out. Many people ask for Uriel's help before making important decisions and he will inspire you to gain spiritual perception that will enable you to live your life in the knowledge of God's laws that lead to a happy and contented life. Wisdom brings us to a higher level of spiritual awareness. Without wisdom it is impossible to learn from life's mistakes but Uriel will bring enlightenment to your soul and help you achieve understanding of your life and the lessons that life brings you.

When we have wisdom and can learn from our mistakes, we are able to grow to our full capabilities and live our life with a deep knowledge and understanding of our spiritual natures. Uriel will shine his light upon you and help you realise your full potential, for with wisdom you cultivate the qualities of compassion and forgiveness, putting behind you negative experiences and bringing you to a place of harmony and peace.

Wisdom is far more than intelligence. Wisdom is a deep knowing of what is right and positive and keeps us free from making harmful mistakes that can cause us distress. Uriel will reveal to you the wisdom of God and will inspire you to seek greater self-expression that comes from a knowing of your true self. This true self is that part of you that is one with God, or the universal intelligence, and when realised will lead to a harmonious way of living and a deeper sense of happiness as you reach your full potential in life. The wisdom that Uriel brings to your soul will empower you to make right decisions concerning your life's path and will bring you the courage to act on those decisions and bring about a more positive lifestyle.

Uriel will bring you a clarity of mind and a deep knowing of what is right for you at this particular time in your life. He will also help you overcome anger and anxiety and other negative emotions that prevent you from discerning wisdom in your life. When you hold on to negative emotions you block the flow of power from Uriel and your higher consciousness that could bring wisdom to your mind. Uriel will assist you in letting go and allowing yourself to experience the wisdom of God that will bring a deep happiness to your soul.

True wisdom is the knowing of spiritual truths; these truths being compassion, altruistic love for all creation, kindness, integrity, and forgiveness, and Uriel will guide you to assert these emotions in your daily life so that you live from your higher consciousness and the divine wisdom of God. Wisdom will bring freedom to your life, for you will be able to let go of many feelings that cause you distress and bring about the true desire for spiritual enlightenment.

The meditation with Uriel will open your mind to the wisdom of God and bring about a realisation of spiritual awareness that will help you cultivate the qualities of the divine. When you align yourself to divine power, you open yourself to positive energies and Uriel will guide you to make right decisions in your life that will lead to greater understanding, happiness, and abundance.

Meditation to Gain Divine Wisdom

Make yourself comfortable and prepare for meditation using the techniques set out in the introduction. Imagine standing before you a beautiful angel dressed in golden robes. This is Uriel, and he radiates a golden light. Feel the power of this light as it enfolds you and permeates every cell of your being. Uriel brings his wisdom to your mind and heart and you know that he will be with you as you make decisions about your life. He will bring you the wisdom of God and the truth of God to enable you to live a happy and prosperous life. Know that your awareness of spiritual truth will develop and grow and that you will reach your full potential with Uriel's help. Spiritual truth will bring an expansion of consciousness that brings wisdom to empower you to live a life rich in happiness and abundance, for divine wisdom will lead you to make right decisions and right actions in your life. Absorb the light of Uriel into your deepest soul and know that you are held in his love. Let the golden light of Uriel flood your entire being and know that from now on your speech and actions will be guided by wisdom in your daily life. Through Uriel you will experience the true meaning of spirituality and will bring this knowledge to all your thoughts and actions. Hold these feelings for as long as you feel comfortable then bring your awareness back to your actual surroundings.

Practice this meditation daily and you will find that you are making decisions that bring only goodness and positivity into your life. Your problems will become easier to handle and eliminate, and through the wisdom of Uriel you will experience a greater happiness and well-being that will bring you to realise your true potential in life. Wisdom is a deep knowing of what is right and you will bring harmony to all situations that cause pain. Your companions will sense that you are a beacon of wisdom and understanding and you will find that you are called upon to help sort out problems that cause distress. Uriel will be beside you to offer his wisdom and love and will give you courage to live your life in the knowledge of God's laws.

Cassiel, the Angel of Saturn

The planet ruler of Capricorn is Saturn and the angel of Saturn is Cassiel, a wise and loving angel who brings his power to the Capricorn soul. Saturn brings to the Capricorn the qualities of a practical, hardworking character with much ambition and determination to succeed. Cassiel will help you as you work to realise your ambitions, also guided as we have seen by Uriel who brings wisdom to make right decisions which will guide you to fulfil your goals.

Saturn brings conscientiousness and devotion to duty to the Capricorn which on the spiritual path helps them realise their true potential as a child of God. Cassiel will help the Capricorn achieve that which you have set your mind upon and will be with you as you see it through to a positive conclusion. The influence of Saturn on the life of the Capricorn is to bring order out of chaos, which again relates to Uriel and his wisdom shining into the darkness of chaos.

Saturn will also inspire Capricorns to bring beauty out of ugliness and peace out of strife through the use of divine power. Cassiel will help you develop those skills through using your wisdom and love for all that is beautiful and peaceful, and he will enable you to use your divine power to bring stability to your life. Cassiel will help you experience the beauty of your spirit and the power that your spirit has. He will bring to your mind the realisation that you are part of God and therefore have great power which can be put to the good of mankind. This power also has a profound effect upon your own life, for it means you can take control of your thoughts and create for yourself the life you want. Cassiel will teach you how to use thought power for the good of mankind and for positive effect in your own life. With this power comes illumination of the soul and the realisation that you are indeed a child of God, or part of the divine intelligence. The influence of Saturn is to bring the self-will into harmony with the divine will and Cassiel will teach you how to bring this about. As you respond to the influence of divine will, it will radiate through you and harmony will manifest in your life and the light of God will shine in your every action and deed. Cassiel will help you respond to the finer aspects of the Saturn power which will bring freedom from restricting karma and a happiness that only comes from a union with God and your true self.

The Saturn influence brings determination to follow the spiritual path of your choice once you have made up your mind. Cassiel will help you to find the right path for your temperament and will help you to follow that path with all the resolve that your Capricorn nature has. That resolve will be the attunement to the divine power within you on a regular basis to discover the secrets of the divine and your reasons for incarnating in the manner in which you have. Cassiel will reveal these secrets to you in meditation. These secrets of the divine are very simply the truth of divine life in that you live your life according to the rules of the divine power. These rules are to be always kind and thoughtful, compassionate, and mindful of the feelings of others. Cassiel will bring to you the secrets of your life and the lessons you have incarnated to learn. Only you, through your life experiences, can know or guess what the lessons are that you desire to learn, and Cassiel will bring about a revelation of the reasons for your life. Once you have learned those lessons harmony comes to your life and a great happiness will come to your soul, for your karma will be realised and you will have found freedom to have control over your life.

The first meditation with Cassiel will help you experience union with the divine will which will bring harmony and peace to your life. When your life is controlled by divine will, only happiness can ensue because you are living in harmony with divine law. Cassiel will shine his light upon you and you will reflect this light in all your actions and speech. Divine will does not mean that you will be prompted to do things you do not want to do; quite the contrary—it means that you will have control over your life through the power of thought. Thoughts are very powerful and have a positive or negative effect on our lives. Divine will is the will of the divine for you to live a happy and prosperous life, and Cassiel will show you how to improve your thoughts and thereby your life through the power of your thought. By imagining what you want out of life, you can bring it into reality with the power of divine will. Cassiel will bring to you the realisation that when you live your life in tune with divine will, true illumination will come to you. True illumination brings the knowledge that God is all there is and that he is in everything and is all love. When we realise this, true happiness will descend on our souls, for we know that we are with God and no harm can come to us.

The second meditation with Cassiel will bring to you the reasons for your incarnation in this particular life and reveal to you which lessons you have chosen to learn. Cassiel will also inspire you to find the right spiritual path to follow; a path that will help you to experience your full potential as a spiritual being. It is a good idea to have a notebook handy after meditation for answers and ideas that come to you from Cassiel.

Meditation to Bring Union with Divine Will and Create the Life You Want

Make yourself comfortable and prepare for meditation as suggested in the introduction. This meditation is to bring union with divine will and to create the life you want to live. Have a symbol ready in your imagination that represents the life you wish to lead, for it will be used during the meditation. Imagine standing before you a magnificent angel clothed in golden robes who emits a soft golden light. This is Cassiel, and he radiates his golden light to enfold you and bring you the power of his love. Feel this golden light flowing through you; mind, body, and soul, and feel its power stimulating your higher self to bring a feeling of inspiration and happiness. Cassiel grants the knowledge that you are one with God and this brings a knowing that all is harmony and peace in your life. Know that divine will rules your thoughts and brings you to a place of wholeness and contentment. Absorb the power of Cassiel as he enfolds you with his love and wisdom and know that he guards your thoughts to eliminate any negativity that can cause so much harm in your life. Cassiel will help you on your journey to achieve your ambitions in life and to experience the life you wish to have. Imagine a symbol of your greatest wish and hold it in the light of Cassiel. He radiates it with his shining light and you know that your ambitions will come to pass and that you will achieve your potential as a spiritual being.

Hold these feelings for as long as you feel comfortable, then bring your awareness back to your actual surroundings. Practice this meditation daily and you will find that your greatest wish will manifest itself in the best possible way. Angels are very powerful and they act out of deep love for humankind. They have the power to make dreams come true, and you will experience your ambitions becoming reality. Cassiel will bring about the flourishing of your talents so that you achieve your full potential in life. Only happiness and prosperity can follow when you work with angels and Cassiel will bring both to your life in the most harmonious way. Believe in Cassiel, for belief is the key to achieving success. He gives you all his love and will bring to your life that extra magic that will enable you to live in happiness, success, and prosperity.

Meditation to Learn the Reasons for Your Incarnation and the Lessons You Have Chosen to Learn

Sit comfortably and prepare for meditation using the techniques set out in the introduction. Imagine standing before you a magnificent angel dressed in golden robes. This is Cassiel, and he radiates a soft golden light. Feel the power of this light as he enfolds you with his love and wisdom. Feel this golden light flowing through you stimulating your mind and bringing a joy to your soul. Know that Cassiel has all the answers to your questions and that he will impart this knowledge through his love. Cassiel knows the reasons for your incarnation and the lessons you have chosen to learn and he brings you this knowledge with his wisdom to set you free and enable you to live a happy and contented life. Feel the light of Cassiel filling you with his love and understanding and know that all will be harmonious in your life. When a lesson is learned it does not repeat itself for you have learned the knowledge it brings. Hold yourself in the light of Cassiel

for as long as you feel comfortable, then bring your awareness back to your actual surroundings.

Keep a notebook and pen handy for answers and knowledge will come to you if not straight away then over the next
few days. Practice this meditation as often as you feel necessary and it will bring you illumination and knowledge that
will fulfil your life and bring you to a place of peace and happiness. When you realise the reasons for your life, you realise
also that you are one with God and as such share his peace,
harmony, and love. Cassiel will bring God's wisdom to your
soul and will bring the realisation to you that your purpose
in life is to realise that you are a child of God and that God is
all love. You realise that nothing can harm you and that you
have the power to direct your life as you want it to be.

11
Aquarius

Gabriel, the Angel of Happiness

The special angel of Aquarius is Gabriel, the angel of happiness. He comes to the Aquarian with his power and wisdom to bring happiness to your soul. Happiness is an elusive emotion but can be gained with the help of angels and a positive lifestyle. The Aquarian soul knows that real happiness cannot be gained through material possessions, and Gabriel brings the knowledge that happiness comes when all is balanced in your life and you have a deep knowing that you are part of the divine whole. Gabriel will guide you to understand that positive thinking brings a relief from anxiety and fears that keep happiness out of your life and will help you practice a positive thinking regimen that brings positive outcomes to your life. This brings real happiness to your soul, for it validates who you are. Positive thinking brings power and control to your life.

When you are happy, you radiate a healing power to all your companions, projecting a positive attitude towards life that can only bring positivity to others. Gabriel will guide you to nurture positive thoughts that bring power to your life. Happiness comes when we have our lives under our control and all is well with our world. Gabriel will teach you how to have control of your life by believing in the divine power that brings us health, happiness, and abundance. Belief is the true secret of a happy life; belief in divine power that brings harmony to your life and peace to your soul. Gabriel will connect you to this divine power and teach you how to always think positively instead of negatively. True happiness occurs when all is harmonious in our lives, and Gabriel will bring this harmony to your life.

Thinking positively means aligning yourself with the great "I am." If you are always saying "I am broke" or "I am miserable," these things will manifest in your life. A positive statement would be "I am part of the divine which is all powerful, therefore I am prosperous and happy. All is harmonious in my life." Gabriel will give you the power to manifest these things and bring you to a state of supreme happiness, for all will be well in your life. When you lack abundance, it is difficult to feel happy because it can promote feelings of anxiety and fear. Gabriel will give you the courage to seek remedies and accept change in your life as well as empower your positive thoughts. When in a state of lack an important affirmation is "I am part of the divine power which is all abundance, therefore I am abundant also." Really believe these words and abundance will come to you and bring happiness once more to your life.

A state of happiness depends on your well-being, and Gabriel will give you his love and power to bring about a profound change in your life. Feelings of happiness uplift us above everyday cares and worries, connecting us to our spiritual self, the part of us that's one with God.

Happiness also depends upon your relationships, and Aquarians are adept at making friendships and staying loyal and true to those friendships. Suffering from problems with a relationship can cause great unhappiness, but Gabriel is there to bring you understanding and his love to your soul. If a relationship is not going well or you have no meaningful relationship in your life at present, Gabriel will help you attain that which you desire. Relationships define us, and when they don't work out well, it can bring much unhappiness. Ask Gabriel in meditation to help you attain your desires, and he will not let you down. He will work his magic in your life and bring happiness to your soul.

Happiness occurs when you are at peace with yourself. Peace comes to your soul when you are fulfilled in your life and your talents are allowed to flourish, giving you a sense of well-being and contentment. Achieving your full potential in life is the surest way to real happiness, so if you feel your talents are underdeveloped you can sometimes feel frustrated and depressed. Those feelings in turn stand in the way of true happiness. Gabriel will bring his power to your soul and lead you to ways of fulfilling the promise of your talents. He will bring you the courage to effect changes in your life that are necessary for expressing your talents to the fullest and experiencing the happiness it brings to your soul. Creativity is not limited to the arts—it can be expressed in all of life's aspects. Through Gabriel, discover your creative talents and use them to their full potential. Gabriel will open your mind to your many talents and gifts, helping you achieve the full potential they bring as well as the harmony and well-being this brings to your life.

Meditation to Understand the True Meaning of Happiness and Achieve Happiness in Your Life

Sit comfortably and prepare for meditation as set out in the introduction. Standing in front of you is a magnificent angel clothed in golden robes. This is Gabriel, and he brings all his love and power to your soul. Gabriel inspires you to honour your talents and bring them to the full potential they are designed to express. Happiness comes from nurturing your talents, and it will radiate from you and inspire others. Feel the love of Gabriel enfolding you in golden light, inspiring you to develop your talents and express yourself in the way you were born to express yourself. The light and power of Gabriel permeates every cell of your being bringing peace and harmony to your soul, a peace and harmony that will bring happiness and joy to your life. Gabriel brings a positive outlook to your mind, as positivity brings harmony to your life and puts you in a position of power. When you realise this power and put it into action, peace and stability come to your soul and you find happiness as a natural part of life. Gabriel's love and power heals relationship problems and brings a new awareness of how to deal with troubled elements in your life. His wisdom inspires you and his love empowers you to deal with problems in the most harmonious and respectful way that brings peace and happiness to you. Enjoy the peace that Gabriel's enfolding light brings to your soul and know that happiness will flourish and grow there. Gabriel radiates his golden light to fill you with power and wisdom. Absorb his wisdom and love, knowing that your thinking will become more positive as you are held in the power of Gabriel. Hold yourself in the golden powerful light of Gabriel and know that all will be well in your life. Happiness will express itself as you go about your life and a deep wisdom will come to your heart and mind.

Hold these feelings for as long as you feel comfortable, then bring your awareness back to your actual surroundings. Practice this meditation daily for as long as you feel necessary, and you will find that happiness becomes a regular part of your life. You will feel yourself lifted above everyday cares and worries to new heights of inspiration and love. You will radiate a joy that inspires others and brings love and new relationships. Gabriel will be beside you when you feel down and bring happiness that comes from the deepest part of your spirit and is a happiness that stays with you whatever your outer circumstances.

Deliel, the Angel of the Magenta Ray

The colour ray of the Aquarian is magenta and the angel of the magenta ray is Deliel. This colour is the colour of the nonconformist and Aquarius is the nonconformist of the zodiac. You like to be different and to surprise people and the colour magenta reflects these traits, and Deliel will bring you the courage to make your own path in life and to fulfil your ambitions and dreams that will bring happiness to your soul.

Magenta is the colour of harmony and common sense, which perfectly suits the Aquarian character, for you are very practical and have a balanced outlook on life. Deliel will bring the power of the magenta ray to the Aquarian soul to bring about harmony in your life and an understanding of spiritual Law. Deliel will encourage the Aquarian soul through the magenta ray to have a balanced view of life and to rise above the dramas of everyday living to a new high of spiritual awareness. The Aquarian will be inspired to search for spiritual truth and practice that spiritual truth in everyday living. He will encourage you to experience greater awareness and knowledge of spiritual matters as well as to inspire others with the harmony such awareness brings.

Magenta is the colour of transformation and Deliel will assist you in healing old emotional scars and patterns and will help you to move forward on the spiritual path. Transformation is the goal of all on the spiritual path and Deliel will bring his power and love to your soul to help you understand the transformation process. Transformation in alchemy means turning base metal into pure gold and in spiritual terms this means turning the earthly personality with its fears and negative aspects into a personality ruled by the goodness of the spirit. Transformation means living life from a spiritual point of view with compassion, honesty, and kindness for all you meet. These qualities are already firmly based in the Aquarian character and Deliel will help you develop them further. When you live from the spirit, you experience a great happiness and joy for you are defining yourself by the highest standards and allowing yourself to live to your full potential.

The colour magenta blends the passion and energy of red with the restrained quiet energy of violet. The Aquarian will find that by dwelling on the colour magenta he/she is drawn out of their dream world when they have become too introspective, a state of being the Aquarian is apt to go into. Deliel will bring his wisdom to the Aquarian, offering inspiration that leads to the greater depths of spiritual knowledge that bring enlightenment to the soul. Enlightenment is the realisation that you are one with all creation and also one with the divine. As part of the divine, you are also part of divine power, and Deliel will enlighten you as to how to use this power for good in your life. Divine power is mind power, and positive thoughts bring only happiness to your life. Deliel will reveal to you that you create your life via your thoughts, and he will assist you to be more positive in your life and thereby create a positive lifestyle.

Magenta will uplift the spirits of the Aquarian when you are feeling depressed, frustrated, or unhappy. Deliel will come to you at such times and bring his healing touch to your soul, lifting you up above the trials and tribulations of everyday life. Aquarians can be prone to depression, but Deliel will bring healing to your mind and body and bring relief from the depressing feelings that grip you and hinder you from fulfilling your goals. Depression limits what you can achieve in life and is like a dark cloud that descends upon you, shutting out the warming light of the sun. Deliel will lift this dark cloud from you and bring you gently back into the sunlight. Deliel's healing is powerful and final and the meditation with Deliel will heal you of depression and bring about a positive and happy outlook on life. When you feel down it is a good idea to have something the colour of magenta to hold or have near you, for it has uplifting qualities that combined with the healing of Deliel, will banish those black clouds forever. Magenta is the colour of happiness, cheerfulness, and contentment, so always having something the colour of magenta on your person will ensure a happy outlook. Deliel will help you appreciate all the good things you have in your life and will encourage you to pursue your dreams with a positive attitude that brings lasting joy and happiness to you.

The magenta ray will bring energy to the Aquarian when you are feeling depleted. The meditation with Deliel will bring renewed vitality to your mind and body when you are feeling exhausted and lift you up to a higher level of awareness. Deliel will bring renewed vigour to your physical being and refresh a tired mind when you have been overworking. It is not easy to cope with life when one is feeling depleted in energy and you cannot function as a harmonious being when fatigued in mind and body. Deliel will restore your energy levels and renew your vision of who you are and where you are going in life.

Our colour angels are always there for us to help when life is not going as we would wish and they bring their positive power to heal difficult situations that hurt and frustrate us. When something goes wrong in your life call on your angel of the magenta ray and he will help you sort it out in the most appropriate way. Deliel will come to you and apply his wisdom to the problem, bringing relief and encouragement that life is getting better and more harmonious.

The first meditation with Deliel will bring about transformation to a true spiritual awareness and bring deeper knowledge of spiritual matters. He will help you live to your full potential as a spiritual being and bring harmony to your mind and soul. Deliel will help you heal old emotional scars that stop you from moving on and realising full transformation.

The second meditation with Deliel will heal depression if you suffer from it. Deliel will bring his healing love to your soul and disperse the dark clouds that block your judgement and stop you from enjoying your life. He will lift you up to a new awareness of joy that depression destroys, bringing to your heart the realisation of all that is good in your life. Deliel will bring appreciation for all God's gifts and release you from the crippling sadness of depression.

The third meditation will bring energy back to your depleted physical being and lift your senses to a new awareness of living life to the fullest. When fatigued in mind and body it is easy to lose sight of your path in life and to lose your vision of where you want to be. Deliel will restore your energy levels and bring a freshness to your mind that will revive your enthusiasm for life and bring about a renewal of your commitment to live your life to its full potential.

The fourth meditation with Deliel will bring healing when things go wrong in your life whether it involves money or another person. He will restore harmony and help you deal with the problem in a positive and reflective manner. Just imagine a symbol of the problem and hold it in the light of Deliel and he will bring his wisdom to heal and resolve and restore peace and happiness to your life.

Meditation to Attain Transformation to a True Spiritual Being and Heal Old Emotional Scars

Make yourself comfortable and prepare for meditation by using the techniques suggested in the introduction. Imagine standing in front of you a magnificent angel dressed in magenta robes and radiating a soft magenta light. This is

Deliel and he enfolds you in his love. Feel his magenta light flowing through your whole being—mind, body, and soul—and opening your heart to the wisdom of the divine and bringing about transformation through divine wisdom to a truly spiritual being. Know that this wisdom will bring fulfilment to your life and will eradicate all that is negative and unworthy in your nature. This wisdom will heal old emotional scars and help you move forward in your life. You will be able to let go of negative feelings and live your life in the wisdom and love of the divine.

Wisdom is knowing and acting upon spiritual truths and conducting your life in a positive manner. Deliel will bring spiritual truths to your heart and help you to live your life through them so that you always act in a compassionate and kindly nature. Such transformation will bring harmony to your life and a radiance that will shine from your heart centre, inspiring everyone you meet. Feel the magenta light of Deliel enfolding you, permeating every cell of your being, bringing divine wisdom to your soul. Hold these feelings for as long as you feel comfortable, then bring your awareness back to your actual surroundings.

Practice this meditation daily and you will find that spiritual truths will come into your mind from Deliel so it is a good idea to have a notebook and pen always handy to write them down. By practising this meditation you will find your life becomes more joyful and peaceful as you come into harmony with divine wisdom. A transformation of your soul will take place, for you will be living your life from the divine wisdom that Deliel brings to you. Deliel will be beside you to offer his help when you feel confused. Just imagine him next to you and ask him questions and you will get a reply. His love and wisdom will enfold you and bring you to a place of deep peace and contentment. True wisdom comes from our experiences in life and Deliel will make you more aware of the lessons such experiences bring. From these lessons come wisdom, and Deliel will inspire you to learn this wisdom and adapt it to your everyday life.

Meditation to Disperse Dark Clouds in Your Soul and Lift You to a New Awareness of Joy

Make sure you are comfortable and prepare yourself for meditation as suggested in the introduction. When you feel ready, imagine standing in front of you a magnificent angel dressed in magenta robes. This is Deliel, and he radiates a soft magenta light. This light enfolds you, and you feel its power as it permeates your being—mind body, and soul. Deliel's power reaches to your very soul where the deep seated seeds of depression are found, and his healing power brings light to the darkness that dwells there. Deliel lifts the dark clouds that cover your true self and fills you with a happiness and inspiration to live your life to the fullest. His power cleanses your mind of negative thoughts that cause depression and brings a new positivity to your outlook on life. Feel Deliel's magenta light filling you with its power and know that all is well in your life and that the dark clouds of depression are lifting. You feel uplifted and healed and ready to face all life's challenges with a positive heart. Know that from this day forth, every day is a day of happiness and inspiration and that the darkness of depression is lifting from your soul.

Hold these thoughts for as long as you feel comfortable, then bring your awareness back to your actual surroundings. Close down your chakras as detailed in the introduction, and take a few sips of water to further ground yourself. Don't forget to put out your candle!

Practice this meditation daily and you will find that the depression that so darkens your soul will gradually lift and you will become healed of this debilitating illness. Your love of life will return and you will find new inspiration for all the things you want to do with your life. Deliel will be beside you to lift you up when you feel down, and he will bring his power to your soul to give you the courage to follow your dreams and live your life to its full potential.

Meditation to Bring Energy to a Tired Mind and Body

Sit comfortably and make yourself ready for meditation by following the suggestions detailed in the introduction. Before you stands a magnificent angel dressed in magenta robes. This is Deliel and he radiates a magenta light. Feel the power of this ray as he enfolds you with his love and the magenta light flows through you. Feel the warmth of the magenta ray as it permeates every cell of your being, bringing a new vitality to your mind and body. Feel the tiredness and lack of energy melting away and an energetic vigour taking their place. Deliel enfolds you with his light and his power brings refreshment to your soul. Feel his power energising you and bringing a new enthusiasm for life. You feel you can cope with anything that life has to offer and you know that from now on your days are filled with happiness, inspiration, and energy. Hold these feelings for as long as it feels comfortable then bring your awareness back to your actual surroundings.

You should feel immediate effects from this meditation, feeling energised and refreshed mentally and physically. Practice the meditation as often as is necessary and you will really feel the benefits. Apathy that comes with mental and bodily fatigue will become a thing of the past, and you will even find that you sleep better, awakening feeling refreshed and ready for anything in the morning.

Meditation to Restore Harmony When Things Go Wrong in Your Life

Make yourself comfortable and prepare for meditation using the techniques suggested in the introduction. Standing before you is a beautiful angel dressed in magenta robes. This is Deliel, and he radiates his magenta light to enfold you in his power. Feel his love and energy filling you and permeating every cell of your being. Imagine a symbol of the problem troubling you. Hold it in your hands. See the magenta light of

Deliel enfolding this symbol in power and peace. Know that the wisdom of Deliel will bring about a sensitive conclusion to the problem that will satisfy all parties.

If the problem is with a person, see this person standing in front of you. Deliel shines his magenta light on you two and holds you both in his love and power. He brings his wisdom to bear on the problem and you know that the problem will be peacefully resolved and that closure will be brought about in the most satisfying way. All is well in your life and Deliel will be beside you to bring his love and wisdom to bear on your troubles. Deliel enfolds you both in his magenta light and eases away tensions and misunderstanding. All is resolved, and you feel relief and happiness that all is well. Hold these feelings for as long as you feel comfortable then bring your awareness back to your actual surroundings.

Practice this meditation until the problem is healed. Deliel's power will bring about a peaceful conclusion to the issues, and you will find all life's problems sort themselves out in a very satisfactory manner. Give thanks to Deliel for his wisdom and help and know that he is always there for you when negative events happen in your life. His love will heal the problem and all will be well in your life.

Cambiel, the Angel of Brotherhood

The special lesson Aquarians have incarnated to learn is that of brotherhood. The angel of brotherhood is Cambiel, and he will reveal the mystery of the true meaning of brotherhood to the Aquarian soul. Cambiel will bring to the Aquarian the knowledge that you are part of the wider family of humankind and are one with all creation. Brotherhood is the feeling of unity with all humanity, for all are struggling upwards towards the light of the divine and all are searching in their own way for knowledge and revelation of their purpose in life.

Cambiel will help you achieve harmony and peace with all you come into contact with, for true brotherhood is living in harmony with everyone that you know and sharing your love and your talents and endeavours with them. Brotherhood brings us into a state of being that reveals that we are worthy and that each of us belongs to a greater whole. Cambiel will bring to your soul the realisation that all are one, sharing this planet in our own individual ways.

Brotherhood also highlights our own individuality. Knowing our faults and good points, our talents and gifts allows us to better understand others. Cambiel will bring into reality the Aquarian gift for true friendship and you will experience the joy and pleasure that friendships bring. Friendships are the start of brotherhood, and by developing your friendships, you are learning about true kinship. Cambiel will bring the realisation that brotherhood is accepting people with all their faults and bringing love to everyone you come into contact with. Brotherhood is reaching out to all, not just those of like-minded persuasions. Cambiel will bring his love and power to you as you endeavour to make brotherhood a commitment in your life.

The meditation with Cambiel will bring to your heart true love for all humanity, and he will teach you how to send this love out into the world to bring healing and angel help to all those in need. Cambiel will bring you into unity with all those worldwide whose prayers are for the healing of humanity. True brotherhood will come about as you send out your love in the knowledge that you are not alone in your work but belong to a brotherhood of those who are committed to bringing their love to help bring healing to mankind where it is so badly needed. In meditation, Cambiel will bring his power to your heart and mind to radiate this love from your deepest spirit. He will give it power to shine forth from your heart centre and unite with the prayers of others who share your goals.

The meditation with Cambiel is a powerful act of brotherhood and will bring enlightenment to your soul, for you will experience divine love at its deepest level. Cambiel will bring to your soul a deep knowledge of your true self, which is one with the divine. Through meditation you will realise your true potential as a child of the divine and your true purpose in life will be revealed. This purpose is to radiate love and healing to mankind and thereby grow in spiritual awareness. Cambiel will be beside you to offer his love and wisdom as you reach upwards for divine inspiration. Through true brotherhood you achieve the ultimate in spiritual perception and Cambiel will bring his power and love to guide you as you reach upwards towards the light of the divine. The meditation with Cambiel will bring to you awareness of your own spirituality and the knowledge that all mankind, whatever outward qualities they display, are somehow trying to reach the same heights of spiritual awareness that you are striving for. Cambiel will bring to your heart the ability to feel unity with all, regardless of their faith and convictions. Such unity will bring a warmth to your heart and open up your spirit to the light of the divine and bring you to a place of spiritual knowledge that you have been seeking.

Meditation to Understand the Mystery of Brotherhood and to Send Light and Love Into the World

Sit comfortably and prepare yourself for meditation as detailed in the introduction. Imagine standing before you a beautiful angel clothed in soft green robes. This is Cambiel, and he radiates his light to enfold you with its power. Feel this power enveloping you and permeating every cell of your being. Cambiel's love fills you and opens your heart centre to the wisdom of the divine. Feel your heart centre respond with a deep love for all mankind. Imagine a glow of light at your heart centre that radiates out from you into the world to bring healing where it is so badly needed. Know that you are joined by all those who have the welfare of mankind as their purpose in life. You are not alone in your work and you know that your light blends with the light of others as they work to alleviate suffering and distress. Know that your light will do good in the world and that Cambiel brings his love to your heart to empower you and brings you the knowledge that you have reached the true state of brotherhood.

Hold these feelings for as long as you feel comfortable, then bring your awareness back to your actual surroundings. Practice this meditation at least once a week to send love and light into the world where it is so badly needed. Cambiel will remain with you as you go about your daily life to help you bring the ideals of brotherhood to your relationships. Such ideals will open yourself to the wisdom of the divine and you will find yourself in a heightened state of spiritual awareness. Such a state of spiritual awareness will bring a joy to your heart and positivity to your thoughts for you will know your self-worth and recognise that worth in others. Cambiel will guide you to live in the service of brotherhood and you will find that your life will flow more easily and all problems will dissolve, for you will be radiating a positive and harmonious power. You will realise the mystery of true kinship and live your life in the knowledge of divine wisdom.

Auriel, the Angel of Uranus

Aquarians come under the influence of Uranus and the angel of Uranus is Auriel. Uranus is the planet of the nonconformist, and just like the power of magenta, the power of Uranus emphasises the nonconformist individuality of the Aquarian. Aquarius is the sign of friendship, independence, and freedom of thought, and Auriel will bring the power of Uranus to the

Aquarian soul to stimulate these qualities and bring them to the fore of the personality.

The power of Uranus is subtle and is felt when some progress has been made to lift the spirit up above the level of pure materialism. Doing your brotherhood meditation and practising brotherhood in your daily life will have lifted the Aquarian very much into the higher realms of spiritual life so the influence of Uranus through Auriel will be profound.

Auriel will bring to the Aquarian soul the teachings of the great masters for Uranus is the planet of divine wisdom and Auriel will impart this wisdom in meditation to the seeking Aquarian soul. Uranus is often called the awakener, for his influence is like a lightning flash of intuition, which comes upon the soul at unexpected moments. Auriel will bring this power to the Aquarian, for the light of Uranus shines like a laser beam through the illusions of materialism of the outer world. The Aquarian will find that sudden insights into the spiritual world will come, and with the help of Auriel these insights will bring you closer to the truth you are seeking.

The influence of Uranus asks us to shake off the old ways and press forward in search of new revelations and new ways of living. Auriel will guide the Aquarian to achieve these goals. The Aquarian character often feels disillusion about the accepted paths of religion and are seeking the divine source of truth unhindered by dogma and outdated ideas. Auriel will guide you to seek a path of spiritual truth that is right for you and will teach you how your thoughts and actions can affect the whole of humankind. Your meditations on kinship will open your mind to the possibilities of deeper meaning of spiritual laws and the role of angels. Auriel will help you realise that the power of angels can bring about significant change in your life. Angels bring spiritual awakening, and with the power of Uranus you will find that spiritual truths come to you out of the blue and bring understanding of spiritual law. This law is that positive thoughts bring about positive happenings in your life and that only you have power over your life. Divine power is within you, and you can use it for good in the world. Auriel will guide you to use this power in keeping with divine love. The brotherhood meditation with Cambiel will awaken your mind and heart to this divine power, and Auriel will take you a step further along the spiritual path to realise the spiritual truth of unity with the divine.

Auriel will awaken your mind to the Uranus influence, which is one of wisdom and responsibility. Auriel will guide you to take responsibility for your life and thoughts through divine wisdom and he will guide you to utilise the power of Uranus for good in your life. On the mental plane, Uranus is very powerful. Only a well-developed soul can withstand the sudden lightning flashes of revelation Uranus brings. This revelation can lead to spiritual and mental confusion for those who are not spiritually developed, but Auriel will dispel your confusion, and his power will bring clear thinking and the knowledge of your true path in life. The meditation on brotherhood will have prepared you for the effect of Uranus, and Auriel will help you absorb the power and wisdom of the planet and bring it into positive effect in your life.

The Aquarian is the individualist and independent thinker and Auriel will guide you to seek out the truth for yourself. You cannot accept what you are told but must experience the truth within your own being. Auriel's power will bring you to a place of deep joy, for when divine truth lights the soul only a feeling of happiness and security follow. The meditation with Auriel will bring you illumination and the spiritual truths that you have been seeking, and he will bring to your soul the wisdom of the divine. Auriel will bring the awakening of the higher self, that part of you that is of the divine spirit and the part of you that never dies. When you live life from the higher spirit you are truly illuminated and live your life to the highest ideals. Under the influence of Uranus, you really begin to know yourself and have some idea of your own special mission in life.

Meditation to Gain Spiritual Revelations and Insights

Sit comfortably and prepare yourself for meditation using the techniques set out in the introduction. When you feel ready, imagine standing before you a magnificent angel dressed in golden robes radiating a golden light. This is Auriel—he brings you all his love. Feel the power of his light as it envelopes you and flows through every part of your being. Auriel brings his wisdom to your mind and his love to your heart and lifts you to a higher level of spiritual awareness. Auriel leads you to illumination of spiritual truths and dispels any confusion that may be in your mind about the right path to follow. He brings clear vision to your mind, and you know that his power will guide you to live your life by spiritual truths and in service of the highest ideals. Such action will bring peace and harmony to your life; you'll find that all problems and disharmony melt away when you live a life based on positive thought and beliefs. Auriel will bring spiritual revelations to you that will help you understand spiritual truths thereby enabling you to live a harmonious and happy life. Absorb the power and wisdom of Auriel as he shines his golden light upon you and feel this power reaching to the depths of your soul. Hold this feeling for as long as is comfortable, then bring your awareness back to your surroundings.

Practice this meditation daily, and you'll find your spiritual awareness growing and that spiritual truths will come into your mind. You will have clarity of vision and know where you are going in life. You will set your own path and live to your ideals. You will have the support of angels, for they are always with you, enfolding you in their love and wisdom. Auriel will bring his power to your soul to give you the confidence to stand fast for your beliefs and the truths that you know in your heart. You will find that you are happier and more content with life, for you will be living from your higher self, that part of you that is part of the divine. All the power of the divine will be flowing through you to bring healing to your life and all humankind. Auriel will guide you to live your life to its full potential; you will experience supreme joy when you live from the divine in your heart.

12
Pisces

Romial, the Angel of Self-Confidence

The special angel of Pisces is Romial, the angel of self-confidence. Pisceans are not gregarious by nature and often hide from the limelight. Self-confidence is often a problem for you and your naturally kindly nature is hidden under layers of damaging self-disapproval. Romial will bring you love and approval of yourself to increase your self-confidence so your many talents can flourish with energy and enthusiasm.

Romial will help you believe in yourself and your gifts, bringing the realisation that you are capable of living a happy and productive life free from fears and anxieties. He will bring to your soul the knowledge that just being is enough and that who you are is a talented child of the universe in every sense, loved and appreciated without limitation or conditions. Romial will bring you his wisdom so you understand that self-confidence is a belief in the divine part of your nature which is in turn, part of the whole. Believing this brings to your being all the power and love of the divine principle. Knowing that your life is blessed by divine love brings a new confidence and ease to your endeavours, and Romial will help you bring to full fruition your unique talents and gifts. Confidence brings inner peace and helps our energy flow in the right direction for the full potential of our personalities to be realised. Romial will help ease away the fears and doubts that surround you and bring self-confidence to your soul as you endeavour to live your life to the fullest. Romial will help you accept yourself as you are and will bring the realisation that confidence confirms the power of divine good that manifests in your heart.

Lack of confidence stems from a belief that you are separate from the one, the divine power of God. Romial will bring the knowledge that you are one with the divine and that angels are beside you to help you realise your full potential and purpose in life.

Lack of confidence leads to a lack of faith in one's abilities and to a failure to fully explore gifts and talents. Romial will heal this lack of faith and restore your belief in yourself as a talented child of the universe. To lack faith in one's self affirms a lack of faith in the divine power that is in all of us. Romial will bring enthusiasm to your endeavours and the knowledge that you are doing your best with a positive attitude that brings fruitful results.

Confidence needs to be built steadily and strongly and comes from a belief in the divine power within you. Romial will help you have trust in the divine and will bring his love to you, a love that is healing and powerful. Romial has a healing touch and will bring to you the knowledge that you are capable of fulfilling your dreams. When you lose sight of your dreams, depression and fear can take hold of your soul, but Romial's love will support you through the darkest times and bring you to a place of acceptance and trust. Confidence will come to you as you believe in Romial and the divine power that guides your life. Romial will give you the courage to look at your dreams and realise the potential of fulfilling them. His power and love will sustain you as you endeavour to put aside the fears of the ego and live your life to your true potential.

Self-confidence comes from a deep belief in the power within you and also a belief in the angels who are there to help you on your life's journey. Romial will bring you knowledge of the divine power within and he will help you to bring energy to your daily life so that you live your life in a positive and enthusiastic way.

There are many ways that a lack of self-confidence manifests itself; maybe you lack confidence in your abilities or you lack confidence when with a crowd of people. Romial will bring you his love and support and help you realise that with the help of angels and the divine power within you are capable of anything. His love will bring the realisation that your talents are gifts from the divine. Through divine love, you can lead a rewarding and positive life. When in company, Romial will be beside you to give you the courage to put in your point of view and join in conversations you may have stepped back from previously. Romial will bring you the knowledge that you are as good as anybody else and that your contribution is worthwhile and of interest.

The symbol for Pisces, two fish swimming in opposite directions, illustrates the choice Pisceans have. You can either swim downstream with a lack of self-confidence to failure or you can swim upstream with self-confidence to a life of abundance and success whereby you fulfil your potential as a talented child of the divine. Swim upstream with the help of Romial and live an enchanted life where you are able to shine and dazzle and you achieve your dearest wish and fulfil your dreams. Pisceans have the choice to hide away or shine like a star, and Romial will encourage you to take up opportunities as they arise in your life and step forward with confidence to a new way of living.

The meditation with Romial will bring self-confidence to your soul and will work in many ways. His healing power will work at a deep level to bring awareness of your natural abilities and at a mental level where thoughts can be negative. Romial will help you as you endeavour to keep your thoughts positive and he will bring about a belief in your potential to fulfil your life's purpose. The meditation with Romial will also work on your emotions where fear and anxiety can wreak havoc with your self-confidence. Knowing that Romial is there for you will eliminate such negative feelings and replace them with trust and knowing in the innate goodness of your being. The meditation will bring a peace to your soul and fill you with a new confidence in your ability to do the best you can and be at peace with yourself. Being at peace with yourself is the first step to building your self-confidence, for you are accepting who you are and what you do. Romial will help you expand this peace until it shines throughout your whole being and brings a confidence that is secure and steadfast.

Meditation to Enable You to Realize Your Unique Talents and Live Life to the Fullest

Make yourself comfortable and prepare yourself for meditation using the suggested techniques explained in the introduction. See standing before you a glorious angel dressed in golden robes and emitting a golden radiance that enfolds you with its power. This is Romial, and his golden ray shines deep into your soul to heal your self-doubt and fears. Feel this ray of golden power permeating every cell of your being and bringing an enthusiasm for life and a deep peace that lifts your confidence in yourself. Romial brings the truth that you are full of goodness and divine power. He grants you the confidence to let this goodness shine forth from you to heal and enchant everyone you meet. Feel Romial's love enfolding you with its power, bringing confidence to follow your dreams. With the help of Romial you will be successful and you will live a life of deep peace and happiness, for you will be realising your own unique talents and using them to the fulfillment of your soul. Romial will bring you the knowledge that it is acceptable to be yourself without self-doubt and that your true self is a radiant child of the universe at one with all you meet. Romial will help you believe in yourself and will bring the knowledge that the life's path you have chosen is right for you and it will bring you success and prosperity. Romial will help you shine as a true child of the divine, and he will bring you happiness and a knowledge that all is well in your world.

Hold these feeling for as long as you feel comfortable, and then bring your awareness back to your actual surroundings. Practice this meditation every day if possible and your self-confidence will gradually grow and you'll see your self-doubt and fears will soon be things of the past. Romial will remain with you to lift you up when doubt creeps into your soul, and he will remind you that it is acceptable to feel good about yourself and to have faith in your talents and gifts. Such positive thinking will bring success and prosperity and you will feel fulfilled and at peace with your world.

Dagymiel, the Angel of the Turquoise Ray

Pisceans are working under the turquoise ray, and the angel of the turquoise ray is Dagymiel, a very wise and loving angel. He will bring his power to the Piscean soul to uplift and encourage you in your daily endeavours.

Turquoise is the colour of communication, in particular, communication between the spirit and the mind. Dagymiel will encourage you to be aware of your spiritual nature and all the goodness that involves and will bring that awareness to your everyday actions and speech. Turquoise is a colour of happiness, and Dagymiel will stimulate your soul to feel the joy of the spirit and enjoy your life, talents, and gifts.

Turquoise is also a very calming colour having the qualities of the colour blue which are peaceful and promote tranquility. It also has the balancing aspect of green and the uplifting energy of yellow. Dagymiel will bring these qualities to your soul and you will benefit from an increased energy particularly in times of stress when Dagymiel will bring his power to help you overcome problems and to feel invigorated and ready to face the world again. The turquoise ray recharges your batteries during times of mental and emotional stress and will bring a gentle invigoration when feeling tired out. The meditation with Dagymiel will bring new vigour to your mind and body and help you view your problems in a clear light that enables you to make good decisions.

Dagymiel will bring tranquility to your soul when life is inharmonious, and he will bring harmony once more to your life, balancing your emotions and uplifting you to a state where you can cope with whatever life offers.

Turquoise brings clarity of thought, so if you are feeling confused about something meditate with Dagymiel and he will bring his wisdom to clear your confusion and see clearly what steps you should be taking. Our thoughts create our life and need to be positive, and Dagymiel will help you keep a positive attitude towards life and will lift your spirits and bring inspiration when you are feeling down. Clarity of thought means knowing where you are heading in life and what steps you need to take to create the life you want. Focusing on the colour turquoise will bring you fresh enthusiasm and courage to create positively and to make decisions that lead you in the right direction. The meditation with Dagymiel will bring you the courage you need and will guide you on your journey.

The turquoise ray brings inner healing of any negative emotions, and Dagymiel's gentle touch will bring understanding and forgiveness where necessary. Simply focusing on something turquoise will bring an inner calm that will help you heal any hurts you have, as turquoise encourages empathy and caring. Dagymiel will bring divine love to your heart, and you will feel a great release when his power melts away any unforgiving thoughts and feelings you may have. Through the power of the turquoise ray you will find life to be far more harmonious and joyful for all negativity will have melted away from your soul. The turquoise ray also helps to build self-esteem and self-approval and this in turn brings understanding and unconditional love for others. Dagymiel will enhance these feelings and bring you to a place where you stay calm in difficult situations and bring your love to heal in times of conflict.

The turquoise ray also stimulates your intuition and makes you more sensitive to spiritual ideas. It encourages spiritual growth and the meditation with Dagymiel will bring about an expansion of your soul and lead you to spiritual enlightenment. Turquoise is the colour of the evolved soul and Dagymiel will bring his wisdom to your mind and his love to your heart that will lead to spiritual awareness of a heightened nature. The meditation with Dagymiel will bring spiritual truths to your mind and these will bring understanding and awareness of your life's purpose. You will find you receive answers to the questions you have about the reasons for your life's experiences, and Dagymiel will bring his power to your soul to encourage you to live life from a spiritual perspective. When living life from the spirit only happiness and joy fill your soul for you have found fulfilment.

The first meditation with Dagymiel will bring renewed energy to your body and mind when you feel worn out and confused. The gentle energy of the turquoise ray will invigorate you and help you live your life to the fullest with enthusiasm and positivity. He will bring a clarity of mind that will help you make the right decisions when faced with conflict.

The second meditation with Dagymiel will bring harmony where there is disharmony and will help you make the right decisions to bring about balance and happiness in your life. Dagymiel's healing power will bring peace to difficult situations and will help dissolve any negative emotions that you are feeling and that do so much harm to your peace of mind. The meditation with Dagymiel will bring divine love to your heart that will bring understanding of others and of yourself. This understanding will promote forgiveness where necessary and bring a joy to your soul, for you will be living from the spirit.

The third meditation with Dagymiel will work on your intuition and spiritual growth. He will bring spiritual truths to your mind and bring you the courage to act on these truths in your daily life, which will in turn bring understanding of your life's purpose. The meditation will enhance your spiritual awareness, bringing fulfilment and a great joy—once you realise the true nature of your being, you feel only joy and happiness.

Meditation to Bring Energy and Clarity of Mind to Make the Right Decisions

Make yourself comfortable and prepare yourself for meditation using the suggested techniques in the introduction. Imagine standing before you a glorious angel dressed in turquoise robes and radiating a turquoise light. This angel is Dagymiel, and he envelops you with his love and energy, an energy that reinvigorates your mind and body. You feel all tensions and tiredness melting away and replaced by a new vigour. Feel the turquoise light of Dagymiel surrounding you, permeating your entire body and mind, bringing determination to live your life to the fullest. Feel the energy of Dagymiel flowing through you bringing vitality to your body and clear thinking to your mind. Dagymiel brings his love to your heart and this love radiates throughout your entire being, bringing a new energy and passion for life. You feel you have the vigour and clarity of mind to deal with your challenges, and the power of Dagymiel brings the certainty that you can make right decisions to bring about a fulfilling and happy life. Hold these feelings for as long as you feel comfortable and then bring your awareness back to your actual surroundings.

Practice this meditation as often as you feel it is necessary and you will find that you have a new energy and enthusiasm for life. Dagymiel will bring his wisdom to your mind and you will have clarity of thought to deal with problems as they arise and the ability to make good decisions so you are living your life to your full potential.

Meditation to Bring Forgiveness Where Forgiveness Is Necessary

Make yourself comfortable and prepare yourself for meditation as suggested in the introduction. Imagine standing before you a beautiful angel dressed in turquoise robes. This is Dagymiel, and he radiates a turquoise light that enfolds you, permeating every part of your being with a vibrant energy. Feel this energy flowing through you bringing his power and wisdom to your mind. This power dispels any confusion that you may be experiencing and you see clearly how to deal with problems. Dagymiel radiates his love and you feel this love shining at your heart centre where it stimulates your soul to understand and feel forgiveness where forgiveness is necessary. Dagymiel brings the opportunity to forgive those who have hurt you and caused distress in your life. Feel the power and love of Dagymiel radiating throughout your entire being, bringing harmony and love where there is anxiety and pain. When you radiate and express harmony a miracle happens and you find that inharmonious situations become healed and love and harmony become a reality in your life.

Hold these feelings for as long as you feel comfortable, and then bring your awareness back to your actual surroundings. Practice this meditation every day to really see a change in your circumstances. Dagymiel will be by your side as you endeavour to bring harmony into your life, and you will find that distressing situations or problems that you have been trying to sort out will heal through the loving care and guidance of Dagymiel.

Meditation to Work on Your Intuition and Spiritual Growth

Make yourself comfortable and warm and prepare yourself for the meditation by using the suggestions in the introduction. See standing before you a beautiful angel dressed in soft turquoise robes and radiating a turquoise light. This is Dagymiel, and he enfolds you in his love. Feel the power of his love flowing all round and through you and reaching deep into your soul. Dagymiel brings his wisdom to your mind and heart, and you know that his power works on your intuition and that such intuition will be enhanced through his active power. Your intuition is a gift from God and you know that you will use it wisely and it will work for good in your life. Feel the turquoise light of Dagymiel enfolding you in his love and wisdom, stimulating your higher self who is one with God. Your higher self knows the secrets of your life, and when stimulated by Dagymiel, will bring this knowledge to your mind. Spiritual truths will be revealed to you, and your consciousness will expand and develop under the guidance of Dagymiel. Feel his power enfolding you and know that all is well in your life. Hold these feelings for as long as they feel comfortable, then bring your awareness back to your actual surroundings.

It is a good idea to always have a notebook and pen handy after this meditation to jot down any spiritual truths that come into your mind. Practice this meditation every day or once a week and you will find your life becomes happier and more harmonious because you will be living from your spiritual self and you will have Dagymiel's guidance to help you make right decisions that are positive for your life. Your intuition will develop and guide you to make good decisions regarding your life choices and this can only bring happiness to your soul. When you live from the highest within you and have the guidance of angels life can only get better and better and you will experience a joy and peace not experienced before. Dagymiel will remain with you as you endeavour to follow your dreams, and he will bring his wisdom to your mind and love to your heart that will bring untold joys to your soul. With Dagymiel beside you, life will become a journey of happiness and joy and you will radiate these feelings thereby attracting positivity and more happiness into your life.

Barchiel, the Angel of Mastery

The lesson Pisceans have incarnated to learn is that of mastery of your emotions. The angel of mastery is Barchiel, who will guide you with his love and wisdom to control your emotions and bring tranquility and happiness to your life. Pisceans are very emotional, leading sometimes to distress and confusion, but with Barchiel's help you will learn to gain mastery over your emotions and bring peace to your soul. When your emotions are out of control, you lose control of your life and decisions you make are sometimes not for your good. When emotions are running high, your mind can become confused and you cannot see the way ahead in a clear and positive manner. Barchiel will bring calm to your emotions and help you see difficult situations in a clear light. His love will bring peace to your soul and guide you to make the right decisions to heal distressing situations.

When emotions such as anger, jealousy, fear, and anxiety take over your soul, it is difficult to keep the contact with your higher self and you lose that wisdom that could sort out difficult situations. The meditation with Barchiel will teach you how to control emotions of a negative nature and bring healing to your mind and soul. He will guide you to contact your higher self and bring about positive solutions to situations that are distressing you.

Mastery over the emotions is one of the hardest lessons to learn, and the Piscean has incarnated to learn this lesson and let the light of their inner spirit shine forth in a clear and powerful manner to heal and uplift humankind. When you are ruled by negative emotions you lose the ability to think clearly and wisely and the bond between the higher and lower self is lost. When emotions are under control the light of the spirit can radiate from the heart centre and bring healing to your life and a happiness that transcends all negativity.

When you are giving out negative vibrations, you will attract to yourself negative conditions which will upset your emotional balance yet more. Barchiel will help you get out of this vicious circle and restore peace and equilibrium to your state of mind. Whenever you feel your emotions getting the better of you—be it fear, anxiety, or anger—stop, take a few deep breaths, and visualise Barchiel enfolding you in his loving light. Feel his love and wisdom penetrating deep into your soul, calming your feelings and bringing a peacefulness back to your life.

The meditation with Barchiel will develop your ability to bring stability to your emotions and give you the courage to rise to the challenges you face. Put your faith in Barchiel to bring his strength and wisdom to your soul, for the road of mastery is a difficult one but one that can be successfully attained with the help of angels. You should not reproach yourself for failing to control your emotions but give thanks that you have this lesson to learn and have compassion for yourself as you struggle to overcome your weaknesses.

With Barchiel by your side, serenity will take the place of unruly emotions. Serenity occurs when our minds and hearts are in accord with our higher self and the wisdom of the divine can permeate our lives so that we live peacefully and positively. Barchiel will guide you to bring serenity into your life and give you the strength to control negative emotions. You will find yourself able to stop and think when your emotions threaten to flare up, able to quiet yourself and allow reason and wisdom to rule your mind and heart.

The meditation with Barchiel will help you bring balance to your life and achieve mastery over your negative emotions. Harmony will be realised in your life, and Barchiel will bring his balancing power to clear your mind and bring your emotions in tune with your higher self. It takes effort to achieve supreme mastery over your emotions, but with Barchiel by your side, you will find that it becomes easier and easier to live a harmonious life free from the negative energies of emotions that disrupt the harmony of your world.

When you feel yourself consumed by negative emotions such as anger, jealousy, or anxiety, take time to envelope yourself in the loving power of Barchiel. With practice, the meditation with Barchiel will gently ease out the negative power of your unruly emotions and you'll find yourself better able to cope with difficult situations. Instead of panic or anger at some occurrence, you will find that Barchiel's wisdom will prevail and you'll find yourself able to handle distressing situations with newfound strength of character and wisdom to heal instead of making them worse.

Meditation to Gain Control Over Disruptive Emotions

Make yourself comfortable and prepare for meditation using the suggestions in the introduction. When you feel ready see standing before you a beautiful angel dressed in magenta robes. This is Barchiel, and magenta is the colour of harmony and emotional balance. Barchiel enfolds you in his calming magenta light and this light penetrates deeply into your soul to soothe uncontrollable emotions and bring a great sense of peace and tranquility to your mind and heart. Feel the light and love of Barchiel enfolding you and bringing you the ability to remain calm in the most distressing of situations. Barchiel's power brings to you the essence of peace and you feel calm and able to cope with all circumstances that come to you. Barchiel teaches you mastery over your emotions, and you know that you now have the power to deal with any situation that occurs with wisdom and love and a calm sense of what is right.

Hold these feelings for as long as is comfortable, then bring your awareness back to your actual surroundings. Practice this meditation every day at first to really gain mastery over your emotions and then once a week or as often as you feel necessary. You will find that you experience a sense of peace and tranquility and a knowing that you can deal with any situation with positive emotion and wisdom. Barchiel will be beside you at such times; just imagine him standing next to you, enfolding you in his magenta light and love. Your emotions will be well balanced and you will find that positive emotions such as love and joy will be enhanced by the tranquility you now feel. You will have achieved that most difficult of lessons on the spiritual path—mastery over your emotions.

Asariel, the Angel of Neptune

Neptune is the ruler of Pisces, and the angel of Neptune is Asariel, a wise and loving angel who will guide the aspiring Piscean on the spiritual path. Neptune is the planet of inspiration, psychic receptivity and spiritual awareness and Asariel will help you work on these areas of your being.

The Neptune ray can either cause spiritual illumination or confusion, but Asariel will guide the Piscean to a wonderful spiritual awakening that will bring wisdom and growth on the spiritual path. He will help you dispel any confusion you have in your mind and find the true path that is right for you. The meditation with Asariel will expand your consciousness to understand spiritual truths, and he will bring wisdom to your mind and altruistic love to your heart, allowing you to reach a pinnacle of spiritual awareness.

Neptune is associated with the sea and the element water has always been associated with the emotions and psychic faculties. Before one can obtain full spiritual illumination you need to have your emotions under control because unruly negative emotions can disrupt the balance of the mind and lead to confusion and a negative lifestyle.

The meditation you have practised with Barchiel, the angel of mastery, is very important as it leads you to the work you can do with Asariel. Indeed, all the work with the Piscean angels lead up to the final work with Asariel and he will enfold you in his love and wisdom to bring you spiritual unfoldment that will answer all your questions and bring a fulfilment that can only come through your work with angels. The meditation with Asariel will develop your psychic gifts in a wise and safe manner and will also bring you to the state of spiritual awareness that you have been seeking. Asariel will bring you to a point of oneness with the divine life and all the positive associations this has. You will experience divine joy and you will radiate a magical aura that has the potential to bring healing to all mankind. Through Asariel the Piscean can send love and light into the world to bring healing to all the difficult situations that abound in the world. This is very worthwhile work and will bring untold pleasure to your heart, for you will be working with the divine part of yourself bringing harmonious expression to your higher self. Asariel will help you rise above the demands of the ego and live to the full from your intuitive self, the divine part of you that knows the secrets of life. Asariel reveals these secrets to you, the greatest of which is that altruistic love genuinely radiated from the heart centre can bring healing not only in your own life but in the lives of others. The influence of Neptune brings glorious visions of eternity, and the Piscean will have no fear of death knowing that the soul lives on to experience greater cosmic consciousness.

Asariel will bring the union of the finite life with the infinite life and this only comes when the soul has attained mastery over the material life. Asariel will help you gain this mastery, and through his help you will find that you glimpse a beauty of the eternal life you never knew existed. Through your endeavours you can bring this knowledge to other souls on the spiritual path and bring inspiration and healing to those in need.

The influence of Neptune brings an awareness of a power greater than yourself, and Asariel will guide you on to greater understanding of the spiritual world and bring rare insight and illumination, making all the hard work worthwhile. It is never wise to force spiritual understanding, but Asariel will guide you to have respect for the unseen worlds and will bring his wisdom to your soul so that you learn gradually and safely of the inner secrets of the divine life.

Through your work with Asariel, you will be in perfect attunement with the divine and find that every thought and action expresses the harmony of the spheres. In other words, all your thoughts and actions will be positive and for the good of yourself and others, and you will live in a state of extreme joy and love for all mankind.

There are two meditations with Asariel, the first expands your consciousness and develops your spiritual awareness. In this meditation, Asariel will help you attain oneness with the divine will and find that extreme joy that only union with the divine can bring.

The second meditation with Asariel will be sending divine love into the world to help heal where there is conflict and distress. This work is the ultimate in spiritual perception and will bring untold joy to your heart, for you will work from the highest in you, that divine part of you that is one with God.

Meditation to Expand Your Consciousness and Develop Your Spiritual Awareness

Make yourself comfortable and prepare for meditation as suggested in the introduction. Imagine standing before you a beautiful angel dressed in soft rose robes radiating a warm violet light. This is Asariel, and he brings his love and power to your soul. Feel the light flowing from him enfolding you and penetrating deep into your innermost being. Asariel's love stimulates your higher self and brings you to a state of heightened spiritual awareness. You feel Asariel's power enfolding you and gently inspiring your higher mind to a higher state of consciousness. Asariel enfolds you in his love and brings his wisdom to your mind, and you know that you will have answers to all your spiritual questions. He brings you to a state of oneness with the divine will and you know that your life will be happier and more harmonious, for you will be living with the awareness of divine love and divine wisdom. This will bring a great joy to your heart, for such power brings about a healing of your soul and you will know the meaning for your life. Asariel will guide you to safely develop your spiritual awareness and teach you the secrets of the divine life so that you continuously live in harmony with all life and achieve a high degree of spiritual enlightenment.

Hold these feelings for as long as you feel comfortable and then bring your awareness back to your actual surroundings. Practice this meditation daily to achieve full oneness with the divine and keep a notebook and pen handy, for you will find that spiritual truths comes to you through the teaching of Asariel. He will heighten your spiritual awareness and you will find that the meditation with him will bring you to a state of love for all creation and a newfound peace and joy in your life.

Meditation to Work From Your Higher Self to Send Love and Healing Into the World

Make yourself comfortable and prepare yourself for meditation as suggested in the introduction. See standing before you a glorious angel dressed in robes of soft rose, the colour of unconditional love and healing. This is Asariel, and he comes to help you send healing into the world. He radiates a soft rose light that enfolds you in love and power, stimulating your heart chakra to unconditional love for all creation. Feel this love flowing throughout your being and radiating into the world. Feel your love expanding, and send this into the world as a healing ray to bless and uplift and bring healing and peace where it is so badly needed. Hold this feeling for as long as you feel comfortable, then bring your awareness back to your actual surroundings.

Give thanks and love to Asariel for his help in this healing work. You will feel extreme joy doing this work, for you are functioning from your highest self and the divine will is working through you. Sending healing into the world is a wonderful way to fulfil your spiritual awareness and your consciousness will expand through doing this work. Practice this meditation once a week or more if you wish, but do it on the same day and at the same time if possible to gain maximum effect for the healing work.

CONCLUSION

Working with angels as set out in this book brings us into direct contact with the divine self, that part of us that is one with the divine power. Angels open our awareness to the mysteries of the divine and lift our consciousness to a higher level of understanding. This brings a deep peace and inspiration to our lives and helps us create the sort of life we would like to be living. Angels bring magic and miracles into our lives and help us realise our dreams. The angels in this book have a double power, for they are working with the ray of our zodiac sign so are attuned to our basic needs. We need confidence to follow our dreams, and angels give us that confidence and help us embrace change and challenges so that our lives become happier and more fulfilling.

Whatever work you choose to do from this book, it will have a profound effect upon your life, for angels will lift you above the mundane and the stresses of your everyday life. The angels will bring you peace and fulfillment and confidence to live your life to the fullest. Angel power will illuminate your whole being as you work more closely with the angels, and you will find that positive things happen in your life as you radiate the love and inspiration of the angels.

The angels in this book will bring hope where there is despair, and love and healing to distressing situations where you feel out of your depth. They will help you solve your problems in the most positive of ways and will bring inspiration to lead a purposeful life. I hope you enjoy your work with the angels for they will bring you happiness and uplifting when you are feeling down. They are always with us and are always there to help us when we need them. Your work with angels will bring a joy to your life and miracles when you least expect them.

APPENDIX

Acrabiel

Star Sign: Scorpio • Angel of the Indigo Ray

Acrabiel is the angel of the indigo ray, which is the ray of the mystic. Acrabiel will guide you to seek the deeper meaning behind the outward appearance of things. He will help you to develop your intuition so that you raise yourself in consciousness to a higher level of spirituality. Acrabiel will also restore your enthusiasm for life when you are feeling low and help you overcome stressful situations and bring you back to a tranquil state.

Adnachiel

Star Sign: Sagittarius • Angel of Sacrifice

The meditation with Adnachiel, the angel of sacrifice, will bring you illumination, for spiritual sacrifice does not mean giving up material possessions, but instead means a letting go of need and the relinquishing of the negative aspects of the lower self. Adnachiel will guide you to surrender the needs of the lower self and live by the love and power of the higher self. This is true sacrifice and it will bring a sense of relief and peace to the heart when you are ruled by your higher spiritual self.

Ambriel
Star Sign: Gemini • Angel of the Yellow Ray

If you suffer from depression, then a meditation on the yellow ray with the angel Ambriel will bring healing to this stressful condition and bring sunshine into your life, revitalising you and helping you realise a new enthusiasm for life. Ambriel is a powerful angel who will bring the joy of the sun to your soul and bring about a clarity of mind that enables you to deal with difficult choices. When you meditate upon it, Ambriel will reveal to you the light within that is all-healing that radiates throughout your mind, body, and soul.

Anael
Star Sign: Taurus • Angel of Venus

If you are facing a difficult situation then the angel of Venus, Anael, is the angel to tune in to, for she will bring peace and harmony to any situation bothering you. Her deep wisdom will guide you to find a positive solution to any problem that occurs in your life and she will bring peace to a troubled heart and mind. Anael is also the angel closely linked to divine mother and she will bring the ray of divine mother to your soul and reveal to you the secrets of divine love. Anael is often seen as a female angel and she will reveal the wisdom of divine mother so that you act and speak with insight and kindliness. This will lift your consciousness to a higher realm, and Anael will bring you spiritual revelations as you endeavour to reach upwards towards the divine.

Ariel
Star Sign: Leo • Angel of the Orange Ray

The angel Ariel, the angel of the orange ray, will bring optimism into your life and a heightened joy that will enable you to lead a contented life. The meditation with the angel Ariel will bring a strength of character that will bring a determination to live your life to the highest ideals. Ariel will also help you deal with distressing situations that upset your mental balance. He will bring about healing and balance to your life.

Asariel
Star Sign: Pisces • Angel of Neptune

If you are seeking to expand your consciousness, the meditation with Asariel, the angel of Neptune will assist you greatly. Asariel will help you rise above the demands of the ego and live life fully under the influence of the divine self, that part of you that is one with the divine. The meditation with Asariel will bring a spiritual awakening and lead you to find answers to questions you may be asking. Spiritual awakening means that you will live your life in a new way that brings happiness and fulfillment to your soul.

Asmodel

Star Sign: Taurus • Angel of Service

Service to mankind is a special part of the spiritual path and the angel Asmodel will bring you a true understanding of service, for it is more than just helping others but is a giving of the light which shines within you and an understanding that all mankind shares that divine light. True service comes from the heart centre, and Asmodel will bring his encouragement to your soul to give of yourself in the highest possible way and bring love and healing where there is distress and peace where there is discord. Through this you will radiate a love with the power to heal your own life as well as those of others.

Auriel

Star Sign: Aquarius • Angel of Uranus

Uranus is the planet of the nonconformist and Auriel will help you embrace your own unique talents that will make your soul flourish and grow. Auriel will bring you intuition, and you will find that meditation with him will bring flashes of insight that answer your questions about the spiritual life. Auriel will help you develop your mind and bring revelations of spiritual truths that bring enlightenment and understanding.

Azrael

Star Sign: Scorpio • Angel of Pluto

The angel of Pluto, Azrael, is the angel of the seeker of mysteries. Azrael will bring to you the secrets of your spirit and the reasons for your incarnation. He will answer all your questions on the spiritual path and guide you with his love and wisdom. Azrael reveals the secrets of alchemy to the seeker, which is the turning of base metal into gold. This means the transformation of the lower earthly self into the golden spiritual being which is our true state; one of compassion, caring, kindness, and always living from the highest ideals.

Barbiel

Star Sign: Scorpio • Angel of Compassion
Barbiel will reveal to you the true meaning of compassion, which is showing understanding and kindness to all you meet no matter what their outward appearance. Through your empathy and compassion for mankind you are drawn to service in some way and Barbiel will guide you to the best course of action that suits your talents and ideals. Barbiel will bring his love and wisdom to your soul that will develop your compassion for all creation and lead you to live a fulfilling and contented life.

Barchiel

Star Sign: Pisces • Angel of Mastery Over Emotions
Mastery over your negative emotions is an important lesson on the spiritual path. Barchiel, the angel of mastery, will help you control your emotions. When your emotions are out of control your life is out of control and it is difficult to make the right decisions, but meditation with Barchiel will calm your feelings and enable you to make the right choices. He will help you gain peace so the inner light of your spirit can

shine forth and enfold you in healing power. Negative emotions will no longer upset your equilibrium.

Betuliel

Star Sign: Virgo • Angel of Commitment

Betuliel, the angel of commitment, will bring to your consciousness the true meaning of commitment, which is a surrender to your higher self and the divine will. When you allow your higher self to rule your life, only positive things happen and you experience real joy and happiness. Betuliel will help you have commitment to live your life to the highest ideals and to the dictates of your higher self. This higher self has only your best interests at heart and will bring you a happier life and healing where necessary.

Cambiel

Star Sign: Aquarius • Angel of Brotherhood

Cambiel, the angel of brotherhood, brings the realisation of the unity between all mankind and all creation, and he will help you focus this brotherhood by sending love and healing into the world where it is so badly needed. Cambiel will help develop your awareness of brotherhood by acting with kindness and understanding towards everyone you meet. Brotherhood is more than just a knowledge of unity, it is a sharing of divine love with humankind. This brings a great sense of fulfillment to the soul and will bring a degree of joy that will lift you to higher realms of spiritual awareness.

Cassiel

Star Sign: Capricorn • Angel of Saturn

The angel of the Saturn, Cassiel, will assist you in developing the kind of life you would like rather then settling for second best. Often in life, we find that we are not living as we would like, but Cassiel will right this and bring magical happiness and fulfilment to your life. In meditation, he will also explain the lessons you have incarnated to learn and will guide you to explore your full potential as a perfect child of God.

Cheial

Star Sign: Virgo • Angel of Serenity

Real joy comes when you live your life from the divine will that resides deep within you and brings serenity to your life. The angel Cheial will help you realise the true meaning of serenity, for it means you have faith in the angels and the divine to look after you and lead you to a rich and fulfilling life. Cheial will lead you to realise that true serenity comes from the deepest part of you, the divine will. He will guide you to live your life by the spiritual principles of love, kindliness, and truth, enabling serenity to become a natural state of your life.

Chesetiel

Star Sign: Sagittarius • Angel of the Gold Ray

If you are suffering from a lack of money the angel Chesetiel of the gold ray will help you to attract riches into your life. The meditation with Chesetiel will guide you to have a positive outlook that will attract wealth and goodness to you, as being in a state of lack is not in the divine plan for you. Chesetiel will also bring to you the wisdom of the divine and will help you to understand spiritual law. When you understand spiritual law, you can live your life in harmony and happiness, for your life will be guided by angels and the divine will. The gold ray represents the warmth of the sun, and if you are feeling despair or depression, the meditation with Chesetiel will lift you up and bring the healing rays of the sun to your soul.

Dagymiel

Star Sign: Pisces • Angel of the Turquoise Ray

If you have a decision to make and don't know which way to go, Dagymiel, the angel of the turquoise ray, will come to your aid. He is an angel who brings the ability to make the right decisions for a happy and peaceful life. Dagymiel will also help you to find forgiveness in your life for when one is unforgiving, one cannot move forward spiritually. He will bring his love and understanding to your heart and bring you the ability to forgive all hurts and wrongs and let go of them, thereby bringing peace and stability to your soul.

Deliel

Star Sign: Aquarius • Angel of the Magenta Ray

Magenta is the colour of transformation. Meditation with Deliel will bring about transformation to a true spiritual being. This means working from the highest in you, and so Deliel will heal old emotional scars and enable you to move forward in life, free from negative influences. Deliel will also bring his healing touch when things go wrong in your life and lift you out of depression and negativity, revealing to you a new awareness of joy.

Gabriel

Star Sign: Cancer • Angel of the Moon

Gabriel, the angel of the moon, will bring divine illumination to your soul and help you to understand the spiritual laws of life. His guiding touch will bring balance to your moods for we can be influenced by the different phases of the moon. Gabriel will bring his wisdom to you to help you deal with life's problems, and he will bring his love to your heart that will bring inspiration and divine wisdom to your soul. Meditation with Gabriel will help you reach great heights of illumination that will bring insight to your soul so you are able to live a more harmonious and rewarding life.

Gabriel

Star Sign: Aquarius • The Angel of Happiness

The angel Gabriel will bring true happiness to your soul and will teach you that happiness comes from belief in the divine power that rules our lives. Gabriel will bring you the message that when we let go of the lower self and embrace our true inner spirit a peace will come to the soul that allows happiness to flourish. Happiness brings a sense of oneness with the divine and reveals to us a state of being that can only come when we are unified with divine love that is the spark of light that dwells deep within us.

Gediel

Star Sign: Capricorn • Angel of the Purple Ray

The purple ray brings a desire to know the meaning behind the everyday happenings of life, and Gediel will bring his wisdom to your soul to understand the reasons for the situations of your life. He will bring about unity between the higher consciousness and the lower self so that you live your life from the highest ideals. Gediel will also help you balance your energies so you do not overwhelm yourself with too much to do.

Hamaliel

Star Sign: Virgo • Angel of the Blue Ray

Meditation with Hamaliel, the angel of the blue ray, will help you to relieve stress in your life and to find contentment and tranquility. Hamaliel will also show you how to communicate your true self, which is a loving shining spirit, in all that you do. When you reveal your true self, you will attract good into your life that will enrich you and bring about enlightenment and joy. Your true self acts upon the truths of spiritual law, and Hamaliel will inspire you to lead your life in truth and enlightenment of the spirit.

Haniel

Star Sign: Leo • Angel of Joy

True joy is hard to come by in this demanding world but Haniel, the angel of joy, will bring you to an understanding of joy through developing your heart centre. It is here that real joy resides and Haniel will flood your whole being with a deep sense of joy that will elevate you to a state of everlasting happiness.

Hasdiel
Star Sign: Libra • Angel of Venus

Hasdiel, the angel of Venus, will help you to develop your talents, and give you the confidence to celebrate them, thereby bringing you a more fulfilling and contented life. Hasdiel will also help you experience and radiate divine love at your heart centre, which will bring healing and enchantment to your life. Through divine love you realise the nature of your true self, your spiritual part of the divine.

Hetiel
Star Sign: Scorpio • Angel of Creativity

Hetiel, the angel of creativity, will give you the confidence to express yourself creatively in all aspects of your life. He will help you find your own unique talents and bring you the opportunity to express them in all your endeavours. He will reveal to you the creative power of your soul that will enable you to face up to and deal with challenges in your life. Creativity comes from the divine, and Hetiel will show how to use divine creativity for good and positive change in your life.

Lehatiel
Star Sign: Taurus • Angel of the Violet Ray

The angel of the violet ray, Lehatiel, will bring new heights of consciousness to your mind and soul and will guide you on the spiritual path to new awareness and illumination.

Lehatiel will help you rise to a new understanding of spiritual laws that will bring rich rewards to your heart and mind. He will bring peace where there is turmoil and love and understanding where there is mistrust. The violet ray is the ray of ceremony and beauty, and Lehatiel will help you appreciate all that is beautiful in your life. This will help you gain spiritual awareness and a joy that permeates all that you do.

Machidiel

Star Sign: Aries • Angel of Renewal

Machidiel will bring to your soul the sense of the renewing power of the divine deep within you and will awaken your spirit to the possibilities that come with renewed growth. He will also bring courage where needed to make necessary decisions or when you are feeling fearful. When afraid it is difficult to make the right decisions for your utmost good, but Machidiel will help you find the divine Wisdom within to bring positive thought to your mind and courage to your heart.

Masniel

Star Sign: Libra • Angel of the Green Ray

The green ray is a ray of harmony and Masniel, the angel of the green ray, will bring balance between your head and your heart. Masniel will balance your emotions and help you realise the peace of your spiritual self. If you are experiencing difficult situations, Masniel is the angel who will help you, as he will bring insight and answers to help you over difficult times. He will also bring you the confidence to live your life as you want to live it. Through his love and power, you will find your life taking on a new meaning.

Medonial
Star Sign: Sagittarius • Angel of Caring

Medonial will bring a special magic to the soul, for he will teach you the true meaning of caring. Caring for others brings a warmth to the heart and opens you to the caring of angels. The angels care for us very deeply and by caring for others you align yourself with the power of the angels. Medonial will help you express your caring nature and embrace the love of the angels, bringing you to a higher state of consciousness.

Michael
Star Sign: Leo • Angel of the Sun

Michael, the angel of the sun, will bring sunshine into your life and this power will strengthen your mental abilities bringing about positive and productive thoughts that create a happy and fulfilled life. Through Michael you will discover the divine light that shines within your heart, and he will assist you to send this light into the world where healing is so badly needed. The strength of your mental powers will determine your success at this work, and the Archangel Michael will bring you his assistance and power as you undertake the task of bringing healing to the world.

Muriel
Star Sign: Cancer • Angel of Peace

Peace is something that everyone longs for, and Muriel will bring tranquility and peace to a troubled soul. The meditation with Muriel will harmonise the earthly personality with the spiritual self. When this happens, a glorious peace envelopes the soul. Such peace will help you think clearly about what needs to be done to create a fulfilling life and will help you see where changes need to be made. Muriel will give you the peace of mind that creates harmony in your life and you will find that life will be more rewarding and happy with his help.

Pheniel

Star Sign: Gemini • Angel of Transformation

Pheniel, the angel of transformation, will bring illumination to your soul, allowing you to realise the true spirit dwelling deep within you. Transformation is more than just change; it is the realisation that you are a shining spirit, a true child of the divine. Through your radiance you can bring peace and healing to your fellow man. Pheniel brings his love to your heart and meditation with him will help you radiate this love to the world, bringing healing and transformation where it is so badly needed. This power will also bring healing to your own life where needed, and you will find that the meditation with Pheniel will transform your life for the better.

Rahmiel

Star Sign: Aries • Angel of Love

Rahmiel will bring his wisdom to your mind and soul to understand the full meaning and possibilities of divine love. Divine love opens us to the wisdom of angels and brings about a great joy to the heart, for we are working from the very highest in us. When we radiate love, we radiate a positive power that attracts good things into our life; we live in harmony and peace in all our dealings.

Raphael

Star Sign: Gemini • Angel of Mercury

The angel of Mercury, Raphael, will bring wisdom that leads to a realisation of heaven whilst still in our earthly bodies. You will discover the true meaning of the divine light that dwells within you and which can bring everlasting joy to your soul. Raphael will bring you the realisation that this divine light shines in all mankind and that therefore you are one with all creation. This knowledge will radiate light throughout your body and soul, and you will find peace and harmony in life. Raphael's love will expand this light within you so that it radiates a healing power throughout your life, bringing an understanding and happiness that truly is a realisation of heaven.

Romial

Star Sign: Pisces • Angel of Self Confidence

The angel Romial will help you find the self-confidence you need to lead a fulfilling and happy life. He will enable you to embrace your special gifts and to believe in yourself as a perfect child of the divine. Self-confidence comes from having faith in the divine and the angels to guide you, and Romial will give you this faith when you meditate with him.

Sachiel

Star Sign: Sagittarius • Angel of Jupiter

Sachiel, the angel of Jupiter, will help you realise oneness with the divine light that dwells within you. The influence of Sachiel in your life will bring about awareness of a higher power behind all things and will bring you the desire to embrace that power and work with it in your everyday life. This will ultimately bring illumination, and Sachiel will guide you to fulfil your endeavours in this respect.

Samael

Star Sign: Aries • Angel of Mars

Samael, the angel of Mars, will bring harmony and guidance to your life so that you live in harmony with your spirit and find balance and positivity in all you do. Samael will bring you wisdom when things go wrong and enable you to proceed with clear thinking and a positive heart. Meditation with Samael will bring spiritual truths that will answer your questions about the spiritual part of you, and he will lead you to a positive and inspirational state of mind.

Sattamiel

Star Sign: Cancer • Angel of the Silver Ray

Sattamiel will help you develop your healing powers, enabling you to help others and bring comfort where needed. This is very rewarding work and will fill you with a joy that cannot be found from material things. If you are very sensitive Sattamiel will bring healing when you feel vulnerable or hurt. Sattamiel will enfold you in his protective power at such times, and you can tune in to his love and support when you are feeling threatened. If you are shy and do make friends easily the meditation with Sattamiel will help you in this respect. His power will bring confidence and you'll find that your relationships blossom with his help.

Shenial

Star Sign: Capricorn • Angel of Pleasure

Shenial, the angel of pleasure, will help you understand pleasure in its true context. Pleasure can put you in touch with your
higher spiritual self and can lift you up when depressing or
negative things are happening in your life. Shenial will help you
see true pleasure as a gift from God that can bring goodness
and inspiration into your life. The meditation with Shenial will
help your spirit soar above the mundane of everyday living and
he will reveal to you the power of the simplest of pleasures.

Suriel

Star Sign: Taurus • Angel of Beauty

Suriel, the angel of beauty, will open your eyes to the true
meaning of beauty and will bring an understanding that all
mankind are at their deepest spiritual level beautiful children
of God. Suriel will help you appreciate the wonderful beauty
of all creation, bringing you to new heights of spiritual awareness. The meditation with Suriel will bring a clearer understanding of your innermost spirit, and this understanding
will illuminate your soul and enrich your spirit.

Teletiel

Star Sign: Aries • Angel of the Red Ray

If you need some energy during April, tune in to the angel
Teletiel, the angel of the red ray, who will energise your mind,
body, and soul. He will also come to your aid when things go
wrong in your life and you encounter problems. His healing
touch will bring harmony and peace to the situation and bring

a positive outlook to your mind. Meditation with Teletiel will reveal to you the deeper mysteries of your spirit, and he will set you on the path of initiation into the meaning of your life.

Tomimiel

Star Sign: Gemini • Angel of Positive Thinking

Tomimiel will bring about a more positive attitude to life in general and will help you train your mind to follow the wisdom of the higher mind, thereby achieving illumination and a clear motivation to lead a positive life. Our thoughts create the life we lead and therefore should be positive in order that we lead the sort of life we want. Negative thoughts create negative conditions, but Tomimiel will help you control your thoughts so they are only positive and for your highest good. With positive thinking, you can create anything you want, and Tomimiel will inspire your creative and rewarding life.

Tzorial

Star Sign: Libra • Angel of Courage

Tzorial, the angel of courage, will give you the courage to follow your dreams and bring them into realisation. Through his guidance you will find it easier to follow your inner spirit and have the faith to put into practice that which you know is right. Courage means accepting the insights and truths that the angels bring you and living your life in accordance with spiritual laws. Meditation with Tzorial will develop your courage, meaning that having faith in the divine will enrich your life. Knowing that the angels are always there to uphold and strengthen you will give you peace.

Uriel

Star Sign: Capricorn • Angel of Wisdom

Uriel will bring the true meaning of wisdom to your soul, for wisdom is far more than intelligence; it is knowing what is right and positive in your life. Uriel will help you have the wisdom to learn from your mistakes and progress along the spiritual path, growing to your full capabilities. Uriel will help you understand what is best for you and will help you grow in wisdom so you are able to deal positively with negative situations, thereby bringing peace and happiness to your life.

Verchiel

Star Sign: Leo • Angel of Faith

The angel Verchiel will bring you to an understanding of faith, which is much more than just believing—it means having trust and confidence in divine power to lead you to a positive and happy life. Verchiel will strengthen your faith and bring his love and understanding to your heart when your resolve weakens. He will bring you back to a positive state of mind where joy and happiness through trust in the divine can rule your heart.

Zadkiel

Star Sign: Virgo • Angel of Mercury

Mercury brings about a growth in consciousness, and its angel, Zadkiel, will help you in meditation to develop your higher consciousness so you achieve a union between the lower mind of earth and the higher mind of the spirit. This enables you to have a clearer understanding of the spiritual life and will bring about a more contented and happier life—when the lower and higher minds are in harmony, it pervades in your daily life. Zadkiel will also bring you messages from the angelic sphere that answer any questions you have about the spiritual path.

Zorial

Star Sign: Cancer • Angel of Imagination

Angels are very powerful beings, but they are hidden from our earthly sight. It is through our imagination that we bring them into reality and absorb their spiritual power. Zorial, the angel of imagination, will help you bring angels into genuine reality. He will also help you keep your imaginings positive, as it is very easy to imagine all sorts of negative things when you are feeling down. Zorial will help you fade negative imaginings from your mind and replace them with positive thought patterns.

Zuriel

Star Sign: Libra • Angel of Harmony

Zuriel will reveal to you the true meaning of harmony and how to achieve it in your daily life. Harmony means living your life true to your inner light, and Zuriel will guide you to listen to the still, small voice within that comes to you from the divine part of yourself. Zuriel will help you find harmony in your being by blending the divine inner spirit in you with your earthly self, which needs to be in balance. When you live your life through your inner spirit, harmony comes to you and you'll find yourself raised in consciousness and living a life of joy and contentment.